Barbados

Fodor's 90

Barbados

Barbara Currie

This book contains material previously published as
Fodor's Fun in Barbados.

FODOR'S TRAVEL PUBLICATIONS, INC.
New York & London

ISBN 0–679–01743–7

Fodor's Barbados

Editor: Vernon Nahrgang
Editorial Contributor: Sandra Hart
Maps: Mark Stein
Illustrations: Michael Kaplan, Ted Burwell
Cover Photograph: Paul Barton

Cover Design: Vignelli Associates

Special Sales

Fodor's Travel Publications are available at special discounts for bulk
purchases (100 copies or more) for sales promotions or premiums.
Special editions, including personalized covers, excerpts of existing
guides, and corporate imprints, can be created in large quantities for
special needs. For more information write to Special Marketing,
Fodor's Travel Publications, 201 East 50th St., New York, NY 10022.
Inquiries from the United Kingdom should be sent to Fodor's Travel
Publications, 30–32 Bedford Square, London WC1B 3SG.

MANUFACTURED IN THE UNITED STATES OF AMERICA
10 9 8 7 6 5 4 3 2 1

Contents

FOREWORD

The beaches, the water sports, the diving, and the resorts capture the attention of many visitors to Barbados, while others look inland as well to the wildlife preserves, the agricultural landscape, the cultural influences, and—the island's greatest treasure—the Barbadians themselves, whether performing in concert or encountered on the streets of Bridgetown.

Fodor's Barbados is a new version of the two-year-old *Fodor's Fun in Barbados,* revised and updated to reflect price changes, the opening of new resort hotels, and the recent popularity or success of restaurants and nightspots.

While every care has been taken to assure the accuracy of the information in this guide, the passage of time will always bring change, and consequently the publisher cannot accept responsibility for errors that may occur.

All prices and opening times quoted here are based on information available to us at press time. Hours and admission fees may change, however, and the prudent traveler will avoid inconvenience by calling ahead.

Fodor's wants to hear about your travel experiences, both pleasant and unpleasant. When a hotel or restaurant fails to live up to its billing, let us know and we will investigate the complaint and revise our entries where the facts warrant it.

Send your letters to the editors of Fodor's Travel Publications, 201 E. 50th Street, New York, NY 10022.

Barbados

Overview

Welcome to Barbados, a gentle land of plenty for almost every traveler seeking an island playground—or an island retreat. This comparatively small, pear-shaped island 1,600 miles southeast of Miami is the far-flung cousin in this family of Caribbean isles called the Windwards, which begin with Martinique and stretch south to Grenada. Barbados's spectacular and diverse coastline never really touches the Caribbean Sea; this is the only truly tropical South Atlantic island. Yet its climate—famous as one of the hemisphere's healthiest—is Caribbean.

THE PEOPLE

What makes Barbados so special is more than its outstanding collection of fine resorts and beautiful beaches, its myriad sports and startling sightseeing attractions. Much of the credit goes to the 260,000 natives of Barbados, who have made this former English colony one of the most stable and advanced countries in the region. Barbadians are among

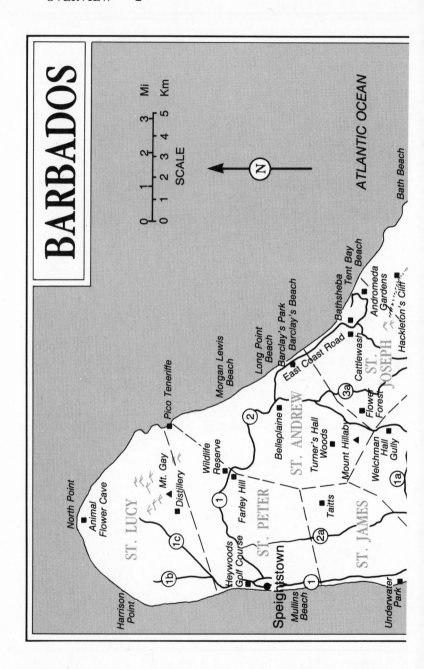

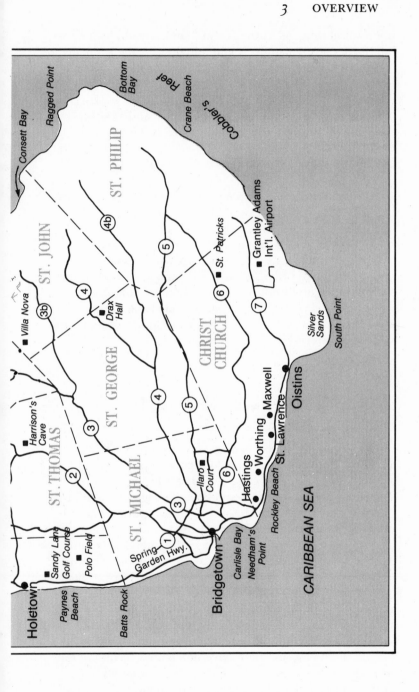

the most likeable of all the island peoples, and you'll have interesting conversations if you mingle with the residents.

They call themselves either Barbadians or Bajans, and, white or black, they share a national pride which both government and private cultural organizations are working to turn into a greater awareness of history and heritage of things Bajan, from music to literature. You'll get a much better idea of the nature of this well-educated population by reading one of the daily newspapers, *The Barbados Advocate* and *The Nation*.

With about 1,600 people per square mile, Barbados is one of the most densely populated countries in the world, but outside of rush hour each morning and afternoon, you'd never think of this as a crowded island.

British influence lives on in Barbadians' innate politeness and love of order. Even the humblest of homes, the traditional chattel houses, are freshly painted and usually surrounded by a colorful garden of some kind. Barbadians keep their island extraordinarily clean, though stray cows sometimes wander along the roadside.

A DIFFERENT DESTINATION

Unlike its neighbors, Barbados is not a volcanic island, but a limestone-and-coral base decorated with panoramas that simply don't belong so close together. On the west, you'll see palm-lined coves that could be in Tobago or Tahiti. In the Scotland District of the interior, you'll drive through tumbling headlands 800 feet above sea level, with a green patchwork of cane and other crops dropping steeply to the Atlantic. On the East Coast Road, craggy bluffs face the tumultuous surf of the windward coast. And in the busy capital port of Bridgetown on the southwest coast, business and duty-free shopping are carried out in the shadow of Lord Nelson's statue in Trafalgar Square.

Today sugar and tourism are the key ingredients of the island's economy, and both have dominated Bajan life for 300 years. Barbados attracted its first "tourists" from Europe, lured by word of its superb, temperate climate and allegedly curative waters on the Atlantic coast of Bathsheba. Legendary Barbados rum—Mount Gay and Cockspur among the most popular—has been undoing the "healthful effects of climate" around the island and around the world for generations.

For over a century, Barbados vied with Jamaica for the title of key colony in Britain's sugar kingdom of the Caribbean. In the 17th and 18th centuries, Barbados was a land of unbelievable wealth, where sugar fortunes were invested in magnificent plantation great houses. It was settlers from Barbados, in fact, who introduced to Charleston, South Carolina, that very style of "English-West Indian" architecture found from Guyana to Jamaica, with traces in South Carolina's low country. History and architecture buffs will find too many sightseeing opportunities in Barbados to explore thoroughly in one visit.

For many people, Barbados will be the perfect destination, one of the most complete holiday islands in the West Indies. With the exception of nude beaches, Club Med-style resorts, and casinos with their accompanying Vegas-style revues, Barbados really does have it all. And while this island may be socially and politically unadventurous, its recreational roster is just the opposite. From parimutuels at the turf track on weekends to parasailing off St. Peter; from scuba diving on dramatic wrecks to rollicking pirate rum-punch bashes offshore on the popular *Jolly Roger* cruises—every activity imaginable awaits you.

At night, you can enjoy a romantic dinner at one of the island's many fine restaurants, then cap off the day with live calypso or steelband music or disco by the water in Bridgetown. Or stay out all night; something's always happening on this island.

HISTORY

Historians believe that an obscure and shortsighted Portuguese explorer named Pedro a Campos discovered the island around 1536. By then, the original inhabitants, the Arawaks, had been frightened away by the rival Carib tribe, and the island was uninhabited and covered by dense forest. Campos allegedly named the island *Los Barbados* ("the bearded ones") after the fig trees draped with mosslike hangings. Barbados remained uninhabited until 1625, when a small party of explorers under Captain John Powell claimed it for Britain. Powell returned two years later to what is now Holetown with the 72 men who made up the first group of colonists. Shortly after, another group of settlers founded Bridgetown, and by 1628 the island was a thriving tobacco- and cotton-producing center.

By the mid-1640s, about 25,000 immigrants had settled in Barbados, primarily from England and South America. A parliament had been set up, dividing the island into the 11 parishes which remain today, and sugarcane had been introduced by Dutch settlers from Brazil, first solely for the production of rum, then as a sugar crop. It was the Dutch cane-growers who erected the hundreds of windmills which are scattered about the island to this day.

Barbados's tranquil past is unique in the Caribbean; in 350 years, it has lived under only two flags—Britain's and, since 1966, its own. The rival European powers, France and the Netherlands, never succeeded in invading Barbados, despite a French stronghold in Martinique, 150 miles away. And Barbados's position at the extreme eastern end of the Caribbean spared it from the hordes of buccaneers who thundered through the West Indies in the 17th century. Nonetheless, from earliest settlement times, forts were built to defend the colony, some 26 of them along one 21-mile stretch of coast. Many of these survive to this day.

By 1670, the population of Barbados had doubled, primarily because the success of the sugar industry necessitated importation of labor. The first wave of laborers were English indentured servants—generally either debtors, nonconformists, or criminals escaping the gallows in return for seven years' service. But these couldn't provide manpower enough, and thousands of West African slaves were imported; by 1680, when the first census was taken, black slaves outnumbered Europeans by more than six to one.

The 17th century was the heyday of sugar production in Barbados, and the island ranked second only to Jamaica in total output. During that period Barbados developed a quintessential tropical aristocracy of about 175 wealthy planter families, who dominated the political, social, and economic life of the island and built dozens of magnificent mansions, estates, and stately homes. Although Barbadian planters, compared with other colonists, treated their slaves well, there were revolts and uprisings as early as 1672, continuing at different intervals until the slaves were freed by Wilberforce from 1834 to 1838.

Disastrous hurricanes in 1780 and 1831 killed hundreds of people and destroyed thousands of acres of crops and many buildings. As a result, few of the early stone sugar-plantation houses remain—the most outstanding examples are St. Nicholas Abbey in St. Peter and Drax Hall in St. George, both pre-1660 Jacobean stately homes. Most of the others along the back roads of Barbados were constructed during the 1831–34 period of rebuilding.

Despite hurricanes and several severe outbreaks of disease, Barbados became one of the first "tourist destinations" in the West Indies because of its healthy climate, and allegedly curative waters. In 1751, George Washington brought his consumptive brother Lawrence to Bridgetown —supposedly to a house at the corner of Bay St. and Chelsea Rd. Lawrence's condition improved dramatically: Washington, ironically, contracted smallpox.

Lord Nelson was stationed here for several years before returning across the Atlantic to the fatal battle at Trafalgar. The statue erected in his honor in Bridgetown is a tribute to a man regarded by 19th-century Barbadians as a hero who made the world safe for their sugar plantocracy's lavish lifestyle.

ENGLISH INFLUENCE

Barbados still produces sugarcane and some of the world's finest rum. But the country that was once called "Little England" by an obscure poet has only lingering traces of Britishness. In 1966, Barbados became an independent nation within the British Commonwealth, and during the past 20 years island leaders have been working hard to encourage a sense of nationalism and pride in their heritage

among the people of Barbados. The current Prime Minister, Erskine Sandiford, succeeded the popular Errol Barrow, who died in office in June 1987.

Some resort hotels enjoy a thriving tourist trade from
Britain, and many still serve afternoon tea. Cricket and soccer are national obsessions, children wear uniforms to
school, driving is on the left, and the judicial system and
governmental structure are patterned on English common
law and parliamentary procedure. Place-names recall those
in the British Isles. Still, this newly independent island is
growing to adulthood quickly, without losing its charm or
its welcoming attitude toward visitors.

General Information

Barbados has been a tourist destination since the 17th century, when English merchants and other international businessmen traveled across the Atlantic and stayed in boarding houses along the south coast. Later, visitors arrived in greater numbers as word of this Windward paradise spread to lands with wretched winters and soggy summers.

THE WEATHER

Barbados's gentle tropical weather is the product of an unusually high number of hours of sunshine, tempered by year-round trade winds from the southeast. Local records claim that Barbados enjoys over 3,000 hours of sunshine annually, with an average rainfall of 59 inches—enough to keep the sugar-cane crops thriving, but not enough to ruin the trips of sun worshippers. Another charm of the climate is low humidity, usually between 57 and 74 per cent (Florida, for example, rates about 80 or higher in summer months). Constant light trade winds keep Barbados cooler in the summer and warmer in the winter than most areas in the region.

You can expect winter temperatures not to dip much below 70–75, with highs in the 80s quite common. Of course, the mercury rises in summer months, to 85 or above. The lowest temperature ever recorded in Barbados was 59 degrees a decade ago.

The lovely climate can have treacherous side effects, however—you'll be very surprised how fast you'll burn. At 13 degrees north latitude, the sun's ray's are intense year-round. Because that breeze coming from the Atlantic tends to cool things off, you might not feel the sun until it's too late. Bring strong sunscreen and sun block for your first few days of tanning or outdoor activities.

Rainy seasons are always a subject of misinformation, evoking fears of roaring monsoons and raging floods. Regardless of which time of year you travel to Barbados, brief showers are frequent, especially between June and November, but even Barbadians are never sure which months are going to be wettest in any given year. Barbados is definitely a year-round destination, and when your whimsy nudges you south, don't hesitate—whether it's February or July.

HEALTH

Not only is the weather divine, and the air pure and clean, but the water on Barbados is also among the world's purest. You don't have to worry about dreaded stomach maladies ruining your holiday, unless you make a habit of indulging in too much Bajan rum.

Barbados's geology is responsible for the purity of its water supply. Rainwater is filtered through the island's coral cap before burrowing through mineral-rich limestone into a series of underground lakes and streams which grow purer as they flow.

A constant supply of good water may surprise you if you associate potability with a profusion of lakes and rivers —surface water is conspicuously absent on this small island. One of the reasons the water is so clear offshore is the absence of runoff to silt up the placid Caribbean.

GEOGRAPHY

Barbados is a very unusual tropical island—it is lovely and green, but not lush, if you associate that word with rain forests and mysterious jungles like those of Dominica and St. Lucia. Barbados is not a volcanic island, but a high-rise coral and limestone mass blessed with some very fertile areas—and some of the most beautiful beaches in the Caribbean. But those wide white-and-pink sand stretches, characteristic of low-lying dry islands like the Bahamas chain, provide on Barbados a startling contrast to the rugged east coast and the undulating plains of sugar cane scattered throughout the island.

Of Barbados's 11 parishes—Christ Church, St. Philip, St. Michael, St. George, St. John, St. Thomas, St. Andrew, St. Joseph, St. James, St. Peter, and St. Lucy—only St. Thomas and St. George are completely landlocked. Only 21 miles long and 14 miles at the widest part of its pear shape, for a total of 166 square miles, this is a small island, considering its wide range of scenery. It is hilly—its highest peak is 1,115-ft. Mt. Hillaby—and the most dramatic views are breathtaking panoramas of the east coast from sites like Farley Hill National Park or Cherry Tree Hill in the Scotland District. From points like these you can see the sweeping landscape, a patchwork of canefields sloping to the rocky Windward coastline.

For decades, Barbados was plugged as a "Little England" by travel writers and some tourism officials, and in certain sections, particularly St. George and the major cane-growing areas, the striking green countryside is somewhat reminiscent of Hampshire and Wiltshire. But in appearance, the similarity ends there. Most of Barbados's lingering Britishness is simply a result of its roots and government structure, and some customs like afternoon tea at better resorts. "Little England" is hardly an accurate nickname for an island with a near-perfect climate, warm Caribbean water, and a people of predominantly African descent.

When you visit Barbados, make sure to leave some time for a trip to the "far side," the long stretches of deserted beach pounded by the breakers of the Atlantic. It's a startling contrast to the Caribbean parishes of St. James and St. Peter. When Barbadians take a break in their own country, they head to Cattlewash or Bathsheba, with their rocky cliffs interrupted by beach, for a change of scenery and climate.

While you're on that side of the island, you can also visit another of Barbados's natural attractions, Andromeda Gardens. If you had any doubts about the fertility of soil or quality of climate, the incredible array of exotic and delicate flora at this private estate overlooking Tent Bay will convince you otherwise.

And in the interior, Turner's Hall Woods and Welchman Hall Gully will provide still another surprising side of Barbados: these are natural preserves of some of the few remaining acres of primeval forest, which once covered most of Barbados.

WHAT TO WEAR

The key words on Barbados are comfort and tastefulness. By nature, Barbadians are conservative; beachwear is *not* appreciated anywhere except at the beach or pool. And even if you arrive by cruise ship, you'll be expected to dress for Bridgetown—short shorts and halter tops for women are not appropriate.

Barbados attracts more than its share of the rich and famous, so you'll see some fashion statements if you look around the resort areas. Particularly in winter months, top restaurants require jackets (sometimes jacket and tie) for men and dresses for women. After-hours wear here is primarily "tropical casual"—colorful cottons for women, slacks and sport shirts for men. And, year-round, there will probably be a night when you'll want to dress up to sample one of the menus of a good restaurant, and maybe go on to a club after. Barbados is not a formal island, or a stuffy one, but it's far more so than most Caribbean destinations. Save the Robinson Crusoe look for the beach.

Breakfast and lunch at your resort will be much less of a concern—many have beachside cafes or restaurants with a come-as-you-are atmosphere. In town, or at independent restaurants away from the public beaches, shorts for men and women are fine.

Regardless of what time of year you come, bring a sweater. If you plan to do any sightseeing, by all means bring a poncho or rain slicker. If you're on a boat, sailing or partying, or driving along the country roads in a mini-moke, you'll find it a great comfort in case of sudden showers. Evenings in Barbados are never cold, but a sweater will be indispensable in air-conditioned restaurants.

WHAT TO PACK

You won't need a converter for your hair dryer or other electric gadgets; Barbados operates on 110 volts AC/50 cycles. But you will need sunscreen, and may want to pack some insect repellent too; at dusk and dawn, mosquitos can be a nuisance.

Since Barbados is such a photogenic country, plan to overestimate your film needs; film is expensive in any resort area and Barbados is no exception.

TIME

Barbados is on Atlantic Time, one hour ahead of the east coast of the U.S.

MONEY MATTERS

The US dollar is worth about $2 BDS, and changing money is no problem at banks, hotel front desks, and the exchange booth at Grantley Adams Airport. Although US currency is readily accepted throughout the island, to avoid confusion when being quoted prices (which are generally in Barbadian, not US dollars) change your money upon arrival. All prices in this book are in US currency, unless otherwise noted.

Traveler's checks and major credit cards are commonly accepted. American Express has an office in the BWIA building in Bridgetown.

GETTING THERE

Barbados's Grantley Adams Airport is served by major airlines from the U.S., the U.K., and Canada and acts as the hub for connecting flights to a number of smaller Caribbean islands.

Airlines change their routes to the Caribbean frequently, and many areas without direct service often have charter flights scheduled, so for an accurate schedule, check with a travel agent. These are the common carriers to Barbados at press time:

Air Canada from Toronto and Montreal
Air Martinique from Fort-de-France
American Airlines from Miami and New York
British Airways from London, with connections to Trinidad, St. Lucia, and Antigua
BWIA from London, New York, Miami, Toronto, Baltimore, Boston, and Caracas, with connecting flights to and from Jamaica, Antigua, Puerto Rico, Haiti, Sint Maarten, St. Lucia, and Grenada
Cruziero from Rio de Janerio
CUBANA from Kingston and Havana
Eastern from Miami and New York
LIAT connects the chain of Leeward and Windward Islands with Barbados
Mustique Airways from Mustique and St. Vincent
Pan Am from Miami and New York
Wardair from Toronto and Montreal

In addition, there are local charter services including *Aero Services* and *Tropic Air,* which offer sightseeing tours and flights to neighboring islands.

Flying time from New York is about 4½ hours; from Miami, about 3½ hours; from Toronto, 5 hours; and from London, 7½ hours.

Cruise ships account for a large percentage of Barbados's annual visitors, and it's one of the most popular ports of call for a number of major cruise lines, as well as a home port for Ocean Lines' *Ocean Princess* which cruises on a varying schedule to the Grenadines, the Orinoco River, and the Windward and Leeward chain as far north as Antigua.

ENTRY

Citizens of the U.S. and Canada must show "some document which satisfactorily establishes their identity": a birth certificate, naturalization papers, or a current passport, as well as an airline ticket home. A driver's license alone is not acceptable proof. Entry is good for six months and visitors must provide a local address for the duration of their stay. No health certificates or proof of any kind of immunization is required from North American citizens or citizens of the U.K.

Barbados has adopted the "red-and-green" clearance system for visitors arriving at Grantley Adams Airport. Those with nothing to declare take the green lane; those with dutiable items line up in the red. Personal belongings —including cameras and sports equipment—are duty-free. Tourists are allowed a liter of alcohol and 200 cigarettes duty-free. You cannot bring in meat (cooked or uncooked), fresh fruit, vegetables, or plants without a permit from the Ministry of Agriculture, Consumer Affairs and Food in Bridgetown (a complicated and time-consuming procedure). Hold on to the slip you will receive upon entering, since you will have to show it when leaving.

TAXIS

If this is your first visit to Barbados, you'll probably enjoy taking a tour of the island before you attempt to explore on your own. If driving on the left in an unfamiliar country intimidates you, you'll find that taxi-tours by the hour are very reasonable if shared with two or three others. Barbados's taxi drivers are a great source of information on where to eat, drink, and shop. You might find that a really entertaining taxi operator is worth more than the hourly rate just for his witty commentary and insights into the way the island works—or doesn't.

If you're traveling alone, or as a couple, taxi fares between points can become expensive, and the fare is not suspended if you ask the driver to wait while you dine, shop, or sightsee. The average waiting rate is $4 per hour.

According to the Barbados Board of Tourism, the approximate rates between key locations are:

Between Grantley Adams Airport and

Bathsheba	$18.00
Bridgetown	$13.00
Crane Beach	$ 9.00
Heywoods	$22.00
Hilton/Grand Bay	$10.00
Holetown	$15.00
St. James resorts	$16.00
Sam Lord's Castle	$10.00

Between Bridgetown Center and

Heywoods	$14.00
Hilton/Grand Bay	$ 3.50
Holetown	$10.00
St. James Resorts	$10.00
St. Lawrence	$ 7.00
Sam Lord's Castle	$17.00

The official hourly rate for taxi hire is $16—settle on the rate at the beginning of your trip, or you may be charged stop by stop. Many taxis charge a flat $75 for a five-hour tour—either you can choose your itinerary by selecting which sights interest you most, or you can leave it up to the driver. You should expect to tip the driver at least 10%, more if you feel his services were outstanding. And it shouldn't be necessary to mention that drivers will be very grateful if you include them in your stops for cold drinks along the way. Remember that admission fees to all attractions are your responsibility.

Many resorts have a fleet of taxi drivers who service

their guests. If you find elsewhere a driver you want to engage, get his phone number—you're not violating any union rules or unspoken ethics by using your own favorite.

TOURS

Several agencies in Barbados offer regular tours of the island, sold either direct through the company or through the activities desk at your hotel.

Custom Tours (425–0099) offers individualized touring that takes people where they want to go. Pickup at 9:30 A.M. in an air-conditioned car, a picnic lunch, and return by 4 P.M. costs $75 for two persons, everything included.

One of the most popular tours is **L.E. Williams** (427–1043), which offers an 80-mile island tour by comfortable bus, with continuous commentary by an entertaining driver/guide. Included in this all-day tour (you will be picked up at your hotel and returned at no extra charge) are free drinks on the bus, a Bajan chicken or fish lunch at the Atlantis Hotel in Bathsheba, and admission to attractions charging a fee. The tour covers Bridgetown's Deep Water Harbour, Bridgetown Center, Sunset Crest (St. James), Speightstown, Animal Flower Cave, Cherry Tree Hill, Morgan Lewis Mill, East Coast Road, Bathsheba, St. John's Church, Ashford Bird Park, Sam Lord's Castle, and Oistins Town.

Overland Safari (436–7534) offers daily trips to Harrison's Cave and the Flower Forest, morning and afternoon, for $25. This operation also offers a special personalized tour by taxi, a round-the-island "Photo Safari" for photographers who want a tour to the most interesting and dramatic sights, with a driver who expects to have to stop frequently and wait while they take their photos. To arrange tours—at hourly rates similar to taxi tours—call a day in advance and discuss an itinerary.

Sunflower Tours (429–8941) has tours Monday, Wednesday, and Friday to Harrison's Cave and the Flower Forest for $25 (including admission and pickup at hotel) and a half-day island tour Tuesday, Thursday, and Saturday for $25.

Tour Operators other than those mentioned above, as well as reliable sources of excellent taxi drivers, include:

Bajan Rep. Services	428–7449
Dear's Garage	426–3200/429–9277
Johnson's Stables	426–4205
Robert Thom Tours	426–1687

24-hour taxi service, including emergency calls, is available from Dear's Garage, but only through their 426–3200 number.

RENTING A CAR

If you plan to rent a car in Barbados, you must present a valid driver's license, and purchase a BDS driver's permit for $5, which is good for one year. You can obtain a permit from any police-department branch (there is one at the airport) or from the car-rental agency. Most firms require drivers to be at least 22 years old, and almost all require a three-day minimum on rentals, especially during winter season. Drivers are required to supply their own gas, which costs about 50¢ per liter—rental cars are delivered with a quarter tank to get you on the road, and gas stations are common along the south and west coasts, but not along East Coast Road or less-traveled country roads, so fill up before you go exploring. In season, it's necessary to make a car rental reservation *at least* a week in advance. Remember: *Drive on the left!* And a special word of caution: at roundabouts on the island, you must yield to the driver on the right, or the person who is already in the circle.

The little, open mini-mokes are the most popular rental vehicles on Barbados. You can expect to pay, on a 3-day minimum rate, $35–$50 per day for a mini-moke or similar Caribbean Cub, $38–$40 for a standard shift car (difficult to find), $40–$45 for an automatic, $50–$65 for an automatic with air-conditioning (not easy to find), and $50 for a six-passenger van (without air-conditioning). If you rent by the week, you usually receive one day free. Insurance (collision-damage waiver) will cost between $25 and $30 per week extra, and a deposit of the full rental charge is required for those without credit cards.

The major car rental agencies on Barbados are:

Barbados Car Rental	428–0960
Dear's Garage	429–9277
Direct Rentals	426–3221
Johnson's Stables	426–5186
National	426–0603
Sunset Crest Rentals	432–1482
Sunny Isle Motors	428–2965/428–8009
L.E. Williams	427–1043/427–6006

Motor scooters and **motor cycles** are available from *Jumbo Motor Cycle Rentals* on the main road in Rockley, Christ Church (426–5689) for about $20 per day (three-day minimum) or $100 a week ($50 deposit). Law requires all cycle riders to wear helmets.

If you really want to experience island-style transportation, mingle with the people, and have an interesting adventure, take the bus. Barbados's national transport system is good, and regularly scheduled **buses** run to most parts of the island. **Minibuses** are privately owned vans that travel between established routes. The cost for both is only BDS 75¢; you must have exact change. Schedule information is available in most hotel lobbies. If you're in Bridgetown and want to catch a bus back to your hotel, the terminals at **Lower Green, Cheapside,** and **Princess Alice Highway** serve the west coast, while the terminals at **Fairchild St.** and **Probyn St.** serve south-coast destinations. There are also buses serving such distant points as Bathsheba and the East Coast Road—ask for information about those routes.

Navigating on your own can be confusing without a map—especially in Bridgetown. Regardless of where you are, don't hesitate to stop and ask for directions if you get lost. Many main routes are marked not by highway or road signs, but by small circular markers reading "Bus Route to City" or "Bus Route Out of City." If you follow them, you'll end up either in Bridgetown or on one of the main high-ways, where you can get your bearings again.

Barbados's seven major highways radiate from Bridge-town. But keep in mind that Barbados has over 900 miles of paved roads, most of them unnamed country lanes. Always allow yourself plenty of time when first getting acquainted with the island's road system, so you don't have to rush through any planned sightseeing excursion.

Between 7:00 and 8:30 A.M., and after about 3:30 P.M. on weekdays, there is a very definite, chaotic rush hour in and around Bridgetown. Fridays are particularly bad; congestion can last all day. If you plan to drive from the west coast to Grantley Adams Airport, keep traffic in mind.

MEDICAL FACILITIES

Bridgetown has a 600-bed hospital with private and general wards, and there are several private clinics on the island. A recompression chamber capable of handling scuba diving accidents, staffed by trained operators from the Eastern Caribbean Safe Diving Association, is located in the Defense Force compound.

MARRY ME IN BARBADOS

Barbados has been a favorite honeymoon destination for decades—now visitors can also get married on the island. New regulations require that the couple have been on the island three days prior to the ceremony and provide birth certificates, a Decree Absolute for those who are divorced, and a death certificate for those who are widowed. Several resorts offer special newlywed vacation packages which include all arrangements, from providing a member of the clergy to baking the wedding cake; Glitter Bay (see *Resorts*) is a good example.

A WORD ABOUT HOTEL RATES

There are often drastic differences between winter season (December-April) rates and summer and various "shoulder season" rates. Reduction in summer months can be as much as 40%. When looking at hotel rates, remember that upon checkout you will be charged an additional 5% government tax and usually 10% service charge on rooms, meals, and bar bill. This often comes as a shock—that extra 15% can mount up quickly.

If you're going on a package tour, make sure you understand exactly what is included—sometimes that last 15% isn't!

TIPPING

A standard 10% gratuity is tacked on to most restaurant and bar tabs. You can leave more if you feel it's justified. When tipping taxi drivers, 10%–15% is customary. Porters and bellmen should receive 50¢ per bag. Leave $1 per day for the maid at the resort, provided the service has been good.

CAMERA ETIQUETTE

When embarking on your sightseeing safaris with cameras, don't shoot at people without first asking their permission. If you don't heed this advice, particularly in rural areas like Oistins, someone may bonk you on the head. Most people will be delighted to cooperate—but ask first. The same applies to people's homes. That lovely chattel house by the roadside might make a beautiful snapshot, but that doesn't make it okay to set up your tripod on the front walk.

DEPARTING

Remember to save BDS $16 or US $8 for your departure tax—and hang on to the slip you received from Immigration when you arrived, as you'll need to turn that in as you exit.

Grantley Adams Airport has a comfortable departure lounge with many duty-free souvenir shops; you can buy your duty-free liquor as you leave, as well as any other last-minute gifts, perfume, jewelry and other items. You can take up to $400 of duty-free goods back to the U.S., provided you have been out of the country at least 48 hours.

FOR INFORMATION

The **Barbados Board of Tourism** will send you free brochures, rates, and other information about their vacation island. In the U.S., write the Barbados Board of Tourism at 800 Second Ave., New York, NY 10017 (tel. 800–221–9831 or 212–986–6516).

While in Barbados, you can contact the Board of Tourism's main office on Harbour Road, Bridgetown, at 427–2623/4. Information booths staffed by Board representatives are located at the airport, in the baggage warehouse at Deep Water Harbour, and on Independence Square in Bridgetown.

SHOPPING

Unless you're a comparison shopper or an incurable duty-free bargain hunter, you should find everything you want in the duty-free stores on Broad St., in the Sunset Crest Shopping Center on Highway 1 in St. James, and in selected resorts. If your only goals in the duty-free category are liquor, perfume, and a few local crafts, you don't even have to use your vacation time shopping; after clearing Immigration at Grantley Adams Airport, you can do your buying in the departure lounge at the same prices as in town. Otherwise, you can do your shopping very easily in a morning on Bridgetown's Broad St. Stores are open from 8 A.M. to 4 P.M.

Regulations governing duty-free purchases have been eased substantially in recent years. Visitors can now purchase duty-free goods over the counter—with the exception of liquor, tobacco products, and electronic equipment—provided they show an airline ticket and travel documents to prove they are visitors. Those items, which must be purchased "in bond," require at least 24-hour advance notice and payment, so they can be delivered to your plane or ship. It is very important that you retain the invoice for any goods purchased, since you must claim your packages from Immigration upon departure by presenting the original invoice.

Harrison's has branches at the Hilton, Marriott's Sam Lord's Castle, Paradise Beach Hotel, Sandy Lane Hotel, Southern Palms, and Grantley Adams Airport. This is the store with the widest range of duty-free goods, particularly fine china and fine crystal (Baccarat, Waterford, Orrefors, etc.); Scandinavian silver; Cartier, Omega, and other watches; camera and optical equipment; and the best selection of French perfumes. It also has a good selection of costume jewelry in enamel, semi-precious stones, and natural materials like shell, black coral, and wood. **Cave-Shepherd** also has a good selection of perfumes and fine jewelry, but the unique attraction of this store (and its branches at Sunset Crest and Heywoods Resort) is its selection of Icelandic wools, Scottish woolens, West Indian Sea Island Cotton fashions, embroidered blouses, and Caribbean batik items from St. Kitts and other islands. **Da Costa's** also has a good selection of duty-free items, and has a branch at Sunset Crest.

Other duty-free bargains on jewelry items may be found on Broad St. in **Correia's Jewellery, Y. De Lima**

Ltd., The Royal Shop, India House in the Mall 34 shopping center off Broad St., and **Maraj & Sons** in the Norman Centre shopping plaza.

If you're looking for Barbadian products to take home, you can't overlook its fine rum. Cockspur VSOR and Mount Gay both cost a fraction of their U.S. price.

Local handicrafts can be found in the **Best of Barbados** shops in Mall 34 in Bridgetown, the Flower Forest boutique, Sandpiper Inn in St. James, Sam Lord's Castle, the Skyway Plaza in Hastings, and the Southern Palm Hotel in St. Lawrence. Each has a selection of gifts and high-quality hand-made souvenirs. Look also for "Caribatik," a collection of Barbadian batik fashions sold only on the island.

You can also find local crafts, such as khus-khus hangers, woven placemats, shell jewelry, and wall hangings at **West Indies Handicrafts** on the first floor of the Norman Centre, and at **Artifacts** in Norman Centre. **Pelican Village,** located near the harbor in Bridgetown on Princess Alice Highway, is a government-sponsored arts-and-crafts center with a variety of stalls and small shops built with tourists in mind. The **I.D.C. Handicraft Division** nearby has one of the best collections of locally made crafts. Many artisans bring their materials with them and work on new pieces in the Village—another attraction for visitors curious about the culture of Barbados. East of Pelican Village is an area called **Temple Yard** where members of the Rastafarian sect create leather crafts; hand-tooled sandals, bags, and belts for men and women are finds here.

The beachfront **Craft Marketplace** at Heywoods Resort in St. Peter is an interesting collection of small shops with imported and local crafts for sale.

Some of the local foodstuffs of Barbados, including various deadly hot sauces and the delicious local Banks beer, are for sale in the departure lounge of Grantley Adams Airport. Frozen flying-fish filets are now packed for export, and have been approved by U.S. Customs. **Flyfish Inc.** is the name of the company selling the Bajan delicacy, and each order comes with a supply of the famous local seasoning blend and recipes for duplicating the dish you enjoyed on the island. Don't try to bring back fresh fruits, seeds, plants, or vegetables—they will be confiscated.

ART GALLERIES

The **Coffee and Cream Gallery,** in St. Lawrence Gap near the Southern Palms Hotel, is a small gallery devoted exclusively to promoting local artists. The place carries a variety of art forms—including a good selection of custom-made jewelry—representing about 40 artists. A novel attraction here: a well-stocked bar with coffee and desserts available too. Open 11 A.M.–5 P.M. Tuesday through Saturday (428–2708).

Queen's Park Gallery, located in Queen's Park, is actually Barbados's largest gallery, with regular month-long exhibitions. Art works are not for sale. Hours are Monday through Friday 10 A.M.–2 P.M. and 3 P.M.–6 P.M. Saturday 2 P.M.–6 P.M. (427–2345).

Origins, at Bridge House in Bridgetown, has a small but interesting offering of original oils, acrylics, watercolors, paper objects, and clay pieces, all by local artists. The well-presented shop also has a smattering of designer wear (426–8522).

At **Greenwich House Antiques and Collectables,** at the top of Trents Hill in Greenwich village, connecting rooms and cottages are crowded with furniture finds, china and pottery pieces, crystal chandeliers, silver, glasses and decanters, mirrors, depression glass, cranberry glass, a few pieces of antique jewelry. Hours are daily 10:30 A.M. to 6 P.M. (432–1169).

The Barbados Museum's **Cunard Gallery** houses an outstanding collection of West Indian paintings and etchings, and an exhibition gallery of local artists that changes on a regular basis. The museum shop sells reproductions of old prints, maps, and paintings (436–1956).

FESTIVALS AND PUBLIC HOLIDAYS

During the annual **Crop Over Festival,** a three-week-long summer celebration in late July and early August, the heritage and nationalistic pride of Barbadians takes precedence over routine daily life. Although revived on a national level only in 1973, the festival dates back to the 19th century, when it marked the successful end of the sugar-cane harvest and a period when the slaves could celebrate. Young cane is usually planted in November and takes 16 to 17 months to mature; harvesting takes place between February and June. By late July, the "crop over," as local dialect has it.

Today, the national festival begins with the ceremonial procession behind the donkey cart carrying the last sticks of cane, but the merriment lasts for three weeks after, concluding on Kadooment Day, the first Monday in August. Dozens of events are planned during that period, from colorful parades in Bridgetown to float competitions and the crowning of a King and Queen of Crop Over, the man and woman who have, allegedly, gathered the most cane that season. But music, and specifically calypso, is the highlight of Crop Over, and calypso competitions have become synonymous with the festival; steel-band music fills the air, and hundreds of brilliantly costumed dancers and revelers fill the streets. During the summer season, musicians and singers compete for the honor of appearing in the "Pic O' De Crop" song finals. That calypso competition has introduced such West Indian music legends as Red Plastic Bag (RPB to his friends), Mighty Gabby, John King, Rita Forrester, and Grynner.

If you can't arrange to visit during Crop Over, you can still discover some special events and traditional Bajan celebrations.

The mid-February **Holetown Festival** is a three-day folk fair—with music, dancing, and parties—celebrating the 1627 arrival of the first English colonists on Barbados. A monument marks the place in Holetown, St. James parish.

Flying fish are the focal point of the springtime **Oistins Fish Festival,** a two-day event which takes place in Oistins, the Christ Church fishing village where the Barbados Charter was signed in 1652, and defeated Royalists pledged allegiance to Oliver Cromwell and the Commonwealth Republican Government. This is a tribute to the fishing industry of Barbados's south coast. A country-fair atmosphere reigns for the two days, and along with music, song, and dance, you can watch fishing-boat races, fish-boning competitions, and arts-and-crafts displays and enjoy lots of traditional Bajan food, including fried flying fish.

Independence Day, November 30, marks the end of the National Independence Festival of the Creative Arts, a two-month cultural festival of music, dance, and drama. Barbados is becoming increasingly attentive to preserving its heritage and educating its young people about the island's history, while encouraging a healthy attitude of national pride. The fireworks once used to celebrate the English Guy Fawkes Day (November 5) are now saved for November 30, the most important holiday in the year.

If you're in Barbados around Christmas or Eastertime, keep your ears open for local craft fairs, bazaars, theater productions, and other special holiday events; there's always something festive cooking around those times, and you may be invited to join in some traditional Barbadian holiday feasts and parties.

Public holidays in Barbados include:

New Year's Day
Errol Barrow's Birthday (January 21)

Good Friday
Easter Sunday
May Day
Whit Monday (May 18)
Kadooment Day (First Monday in August)
United Nations Day (October 6)
Independence Day (November 30)
Christmas Day
Boxing Day (December 26)

BEYOND BARBADOS: EXCURSIONS TO OTHER ISLANDS

Barbados is the gateway to the lower Caribbean, and many of the Windward Isles are so accessible you could easily combine several into an island-hopping holiday if you have time. In this part of the Caribbean, island countries may be close together, but their cultures and landscapes are startlingly different. Martinique, Dominica, Grenada, and Tobago all lie within 200 miles of Barbados, with St. Lucia and St. Vincent only about 100 miles northwest and due west respectively.

Caribbean Safari Tours (427–5100) offers a variety of fly or fly-and-sail excursions to neighbor islands from Barbados. These trips start at over $210 per person for one-day flightseeing or fly-and-sail excursions, which include lunch and transportation, taxes, and complimentary drink. On Tuesdays, Thursdays, and Fridays there is an exciting two-day fly-and-sail trip to the Grenadines, an idyllic necklace of tiny islands stretching for 175 miles, including the exclusive resorts of Palm Island and Mustique.

Caribbean Safari Tours also offers a program of Caribbean cruises launched by Ocean Cruise Lines. These seven-day cruises aboard the cruise ship *Ocean Islander* and the luxury yacht *Carib Islander* depart weekly from Bridgetown for cruises of three or more days.

Cruise schedules on the two Ocean Cruise Lines ships berthed in Barbados change each season, and may include exotic trips down Venezuela's jungle-lined Orinoco River, or stops in Tobago or the Grenadines. If you plan to take one of these extended tours, check with your travel agent to determine the schedules that season, and the entry requirements for each country other than Barbados. Tobago, for example, now requires a passport and visa for all visitors.

Caribbean Safari Tours arranges overnight air/land packages to San Juan and St. Maarten for gambling and shopping, and longer tours to Caracas, Venezuela.

Grenadine Tours (428–1639) offers a day of land, sea, and air touring that begins with a flight to Mustique and a zip around Mustique by Minimoke, then another short flight to Union Island for a powerboat trip to Mayreau, with time for swimming, snorkeling, and lunch before the anchor is lifted. Another short cruise to the Tobago Cays for beaching and sun-basking is followed by a return flight to Barbados.

LIAT (Leeward Islands Air Transport) operates an inter-island service connecting 25 Caribbean destinations with San Juan in the north and Caracas in the south. Their fleet of two dozen modern Super 748's, Dash 8's, and Twin Otter aircraft offers regular flights. Be sure to check with your travel agent. From time to time, LIAT offers exceptional airfare bargains on 30-day unlimited travel to any of its destinations (436–6224).

TELEPHONES

The area code for Barbados is 809, and the direct dial telephone system equals that of any world capital.

TIPS FOR BRITISH TRAVELERS

GOVERNMENT TOURIST OFFICES

Contact the **Barbados Board of Tourism** (263 Tottenham Court Rd., London W1P 9AA, tel. 01/636–0090) for brochures and tourist information.

PASSPORTS AND VISAS

You will need a valid passport (cost: £15). British citizens are not required to have visas.

CUSTOMS

Visitors of 18 or over can take in 200 cigarettes or 100 cigarillos or 50 cigars or 250 grams of tobacco; one liter of alcohol; 150 grams of perfume; and duty-free gifts to a value of £30.

Returning to the UK, you may bring home, if you are 18 or over: (1) 200 cigarettes or 100 cigarillos or 50 cigars or 250 grams of tobacco; (2) one liter of alcohol; (3) 150 grams of perfume; and (4) duty-free gifts to a value of £30.

INSURANCE

We recommend that to cover health and motoring mishaps, you insure yourself with **Europ Assistance** (252 High St., Croydon, Surrey CRO 1NF, tel. 01/680–1234). It is also wise to take out insurance to cover the loss of baggage (although check that such loss isn't already covered in any existing homeowner's policies you may have). Trip-cancellation insurance is another wise buy. **The Association of British Insurers** (Aldermary House, Queen St., London EC4N 1TT, tel. 01/248–4477) will give comprehensive advice on all aspects of vacation insurance.

TOUR OPERATORS

Here is just a selection of companies offering packages to Barbados. Contact your travel agent for the latest information.

Caribbean Connection (Concorde House, Forest St., Chester, Cheshire CH1 1RQ, tel. 0244/41131) arranges seven-night stays in a variety of Barbados hotels with prices ranging from £580 to £1205. For a 14-night stay, the prices range from £710 to £1840.

Kuoni Travel Ltd (Kuoni House, Dorking, Surrey RH5 4AZ, tel. 0306/740500) offers packages for seven nights ranging in price from £598 to £1170; it also has a "Tailor Made" department, which can help you plan your own packages.

Tradewinds Faraway Holidays (Station House, 81/83 Fulham High St., London SW6 3JP, tel. 01/731–8000) has trips ranging from £659 to £1372 for seven nights.

Airfares

Both **British West Indian Airways** and **British Airways** fly direct to Barbados. APEX fares range from £464 to £545. A number of smaller airlines, including **Crown Air** and **LIAT,** connect Barbados with other Caribbean Islands.

Thomas Cook LTD can often book you on very inexpensive flights (their fare to Barbados is £400). Ring the Thomas Cook branch nearest you and ask to be put through to the "Airfare Warehouse."

Also check the small ads in Sunday newspapers and magazines, such as *Time Out.* You should be able to pick up something at rock-bottom prices, especially if you're flexible about your dates of travel.

Sightseeing

Bridgetown, Barbados's capital, despite its 100,000 inhabitants, is anything but a cosmopolitan center. With a few exceptions, like small nightclubs along the waterfront, it's a daytime city, and the earlier you go into town on weekdays, the more enjoyable your visit will be, as you'll miss the mid-day heat and gathering crowds—particularly on days when cruise ships are in port.

BRIDGETOWN

Most people go to Bridgetown either to shop in the duty-free stores along Broad St. or to sightsee. If you're interested in photographing the historic buildings and sites, you might visit on Sunday, when the streets are empty, casual strolling is easy, and Bridgetown is at its most photogenic.

Take along a map on your first visit. Bridgetown is a maze of tortuous one-way streets and it's easy to lose your bearings. Parking is difficult except on Sundays. Consider taking a taxi or the local bus when you visit town—both are easy to find when you're ready to return to your hotel, although buses can be crowded and may not stop during the rush hour.

Whether you arrive by cruise ship or car, you'll enter the heart of Bridgetown from the deep-water harbor along Princess Alice Highway, passing by **Pelican Village,** a sprawling complex of stalls and craft displays. To the east, the highway becomes Hinck's St. On the left, at the end of Cumberland St., is the 19th-century **St. Mary's Church,** whose churchyard contains the graves of some famous Barbadian residents.

Heading east after leaving the churchyard on Cheapside, you'll cross Prince Alfred St. and enter Broad St., the heart of the shopping district. A few blocks east you'll cross Prince William Henry St., named after the popular prince who visited in 1786 and later became King William IV. From there, Broad St. leads directly into the heart of Bridgetown to Trafalgar Square and the statue of Lord Horatio Nelson.

Trafalgar Square was established in 1806 on private property which was once the site of Egleton's Green, the town meeting place, later purchased by the Government. Nelson was based in Barbados as a 19-year-old lieutenant in 1777, and did not leave until 1805, a few months before the battle of Trafalgar. The green was renamed Trafalgar Square in his honor shortly after news of his death reached Barbados in December 1805. The statue, created by Sir Richard Westmacott, was erected in 1813—27 years before the monument of the same name in London was completed. Also in Trafalgar Square are the **Fountain Gardens,** built in 1865 to commemorate the introduction of running water to Bridgetown; the park was established in 1882.

Just 200 yards off Broad Street, the **Barbados Syna-**

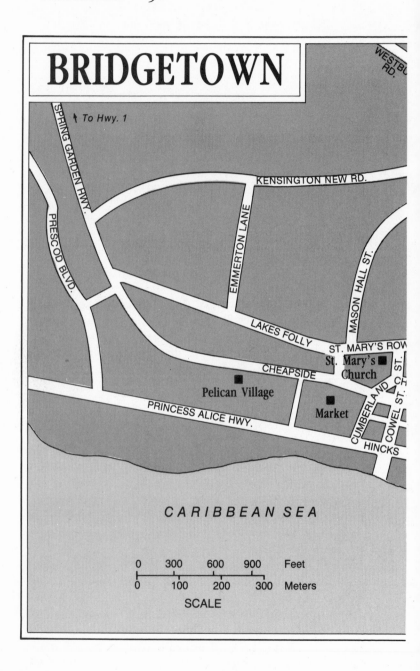

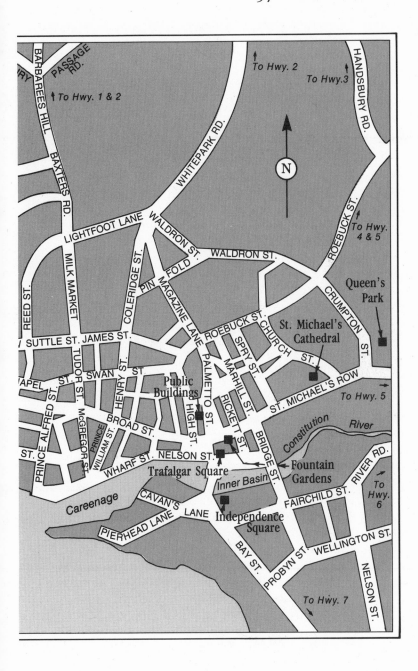

gogue, built in 1661 and the oldest synagogue in the west, is undergoing a complete restoration scheduled for completion in the early 1990s.

North of Trafalgar Square are the **Public Buildings,** built to replace a section of the city destroyed in the devastating fire of 1860. The West Wing opened in 1872 and the East Wing, containing the **Houses of Parliament,** opened two years later. The House of Assembly has some very interesting features, including a series of stained-glass windows depicting English sovereigns from King James I to Queen Victoria and an elaborate Speaker's Chair presented as a gift by the government of India.

Four blocks east on St. Michael's Row is **St. Michael's Cathedral,** an Anglican church noted for its splendid architecture.

South of Trafalgar Square is the **Careenage,** the small, original harbor of Bridgetown spanned by the Charles Duncan O'Neal and the Joseph Chamberlain bridges. Its name comes from the services the harbor provided for schooners a century ago, when they pulled into port to be "careened," or tipped, for the painting and repair of their hulls. The warehouses on both sides retain their 19th-century appearance, making this section of Bridgetown excellent for photography. This was the busiest section of Bridgetown for 300 years, until the new deep-water port at the western edge opened as the island's port of entry. It is still a popular docking place for visiting yachtsmen, who frequent the small restaurants and cafes at dockside. The **Waterfront Cafe,** a particularly nice waterside stop for breakfast, lunch or cold drinks, is also an "in" nightspot, with jazz groups and reggae musicians often performing until dawn.

Five minutes' walk east on St. Michael's Row, Constitution Rd. leads to **Queen's Park,** a lovely public park which was once the residence of the commanding general of the British troops in the West Indies. The highlight of the grounds is one of the largest trees in Barbados, a 63-foot-wide baobab tree estimated to be over 1,000 years old.

If you still have the energy, you can walk or take a taxi—from the taxi stand just south of Trafalgar Square—back across Chamberlain Bridge to Bay St. (Highway 7). About ¾ mile south, turn right into **Aquatic Gap,** a small road which leads to Gravesend Beach; **Grand Barbados Beach Resort,** Carlisle Bay; and **Needhams Point,** where the Barbados Hilton rises on the site which was once Charles Fort. Behind the Hilton grounds is the **Military Cemetery.** The Aquatic Gap area is worth a day's outing, with a variety of resort facilities, water sports, and restaurants within easy walking distance.

East of Highway 7, **Garrison Savannah** is a large grassland which was used in colonial times as a parade ground for British troops. Today, it has a grass racetrack and is the home of horse racing, rugby matches, cricket matches, and a variety of year-round sporting events. Behind the Garrison Savannah, at the northern end of the buildings on its perimeter, is the **Barbados Museum** (see *Historic Barbados*).

CHRIST CHURCH (THE SOUTH COAST)

South of Bridgetown on Highway 7, Christ Church parish, including the towns of Hastings, Worthing, St. Lawrence, and Maxwell, makes an ideal day-trip for those with their own transportation; many charming and out-of-the-way spots line the narrow roads branching off the main highway.

This is also a good way to scout dining spots. There are several dozen restaurants in this informal resort area, including some of the island's best: **Ile de France** in the Windsor Arms Hotel and the small **Ocean View Hotel,** both in Hastings; the beachside **David's Place,** a find, and the traditional "in" restaurant, **Josef's** both in St. Lawrence. Beachfront bistros such as **T.G.I. Boomers,** in St. Lawrence Gap, are more for drinking than dining. Clusters of small hotels, resort apartments, boutiques, and bars crowd the stretch leading to Oistins, and it's fun to go at your own pace, exploring those streets that lead back to the Caribbean and often reveal surprising finds.

Keep in mind, too, the very special restaurants of St. James: **Raffles** in Holetown, **La Cage aux Folles** in Paynes Bay, and the **Treasure Beach Hotel** in Paynes Bay, which turns out gourmet-quality dinners consistently.

Not all the hotels down here are small and quaint. The **Divi Southwinds Beach Hotel** in St. Lawrence is a 166-room beachfront resort set in 20 beautifully landscaped acres, on its own half-mile stretch of beach. It has an excellent scuba diving and water-sports operation, **Underwater Barbados,** several fine restaurants, and a shopping arcade. Another popular larger hotel is the **Best Western Sandy Beach** in Worthing, with 88 rooms and good water sports on a fine beach. Both resorts will give you a good view of vacation lifestyles on this part of Barbados, which is quite different from the trendier west-coast resorts.

St. Lawrence Gap, actually a cul-de-sac off Highway 7, has become a favorite area for visitors to pub-hop and people-watch—there are several informal watering holes in this waterfront area which welcome everyone from early opening time until very late.

A good end to a day's tour along this coast will leave you in the fishing community of **Oistins** around 4:30 when the fishing fleet unloads its haul of flying fish. The afternoon spectacle is a local event which will give you a real taste of Barbadian life. If you have kitchen facilities, pick up a supply of fresh flying fish. Buy it fileted; flying fish is almost impossible to bone.

Nearby is the famous **Christ Church Parish Church,** and the churchyard containing the mysterious **Chase Vault.**

THE SOUTHEAST COAST
TO ST. PHILIP

Poking around this part of the island will provide some beautiful and unexpected views of rugged cliffs and secluded coves. Just east of Oistins, Enterprise Road runs along the coast to South Point, with a forest of sweetbriar and machineel trees leading to the windswept dunes at Silver Sands. You can enjoy this scenery while stopping for a drink or snack at either the **Silver Sands** or **Arawak Inn** resorts.

From here, you'll travel along Ealing Grove to Chancery Lane to Paragon, south of Grantley Adams Airport; the coastal views here stretch along four miles of dramatic rocky cliffs and small sandy coves between Long Bay and Foul Bay.

To reach **Foul Bay,** return to Highway 7 and, continuing east past Penny Hole, take a side road leading south. This is one of the most popular beaches on the southeast coast, confined on both sides of the bay by high, rocky cliffs.

A few miles beyond Foul Bay is **Crane Beach.** The **Crane Beach Hotel,** perched on a cliff high over the Atlantic, is a lovely place to stop for lunch and a swim at the magnificent beach below. Now the oldest resort on Barbados, the Crane will add 100 rooms for the start of the 1990 season, all done in Mediterranean architecture. This property has long benefited from its location in one of the "most healthful places" in the Caribbean. The constant sea breezes from the southeast, a long beach for strolling, and the brisk Atlantic waters are certainly an invigorating combination. At night, floodlights dramatize the beach below the cliffs—definitely the place for a nightcap.

Once again, a warning: when swimming on the Atlantic Coast, never go alone, and if the water is rough, use common sense and don't go in above your waist—treacherous currents, hidden rocks, and unexpected high waves can be very dangerous.

North along Highway N—a short extension of Highway 7—and Bel Air Road is **Sam Lord's Castle.** Before actually reaching this Marriott's resort, you may want to turn left at Robinsons, then right at Wellhouse beyond Harrismith and down Bottom Bay Road. All this meandering will reward you with a view of coastline unlike any other on Barbados, with the magnificent coves of Palmetto Bay, Bottom Bay, and Cave Bay, each a fine sandy beach enclosed by high cliffs.

Non-guests pay $1.50 to tour the manor house of Sam Lord's Castle. Marriott has restored the elaborately decorated interior and preserved many of the antique furnishings, including the crystal chandeliers, intricate woodwork, and the four-poster mahogany bed which allegedly belonged to Sam Lord himself. You'll be told the legend of Lord's wrecking practices on nearby Cobblers Reef—but historians claim the infamous planter was not in Barbados when those incidents were said to have occurred.

If you're planning an entire day's outing along the southeast coast, consider bringing a change of clothes and staying for a swim. The **Cobblers Reef** requires advance reservations and is well worth the trouble, for this is one of Barbados's finest resorts; its garden-covered grounds and lovely beaches are themselves one of the island's outstanding scenic attractions. Lunch, high tea, and dinner here are worth planning for.

OTHER ATTRACTIONS IN ST. PHILIP

If you're still ready for more sightseeing, return north from Sam Lord's to the road you turned from, and head northeast to **Ragged Point,** where you'll see the lighthouse and a spectacular view of the Atlantic. From there, head west, back to Highway 4B. You'll pass the **Oughterson House,** a small "wildlife park" which opened in 1983 and is still expanding. The grounds contain a variety of local flora and exhibits of caged green monkeys, tropical birds, snakes, turtles, rabbits, ducks, and sheep. It is open daily from 9 A.M.–5 P.M.; $1 admission.

After you pass **St. Philip Parish Church,** turn off on the road leading south which will take you to the **Sunbury Plantation House and Museum.** The road leads to Highway 5 and from there back into Bridgetown.

ATTRACTIONS IN ST. GEORGE AND ST. JOHN

Highway 4 is the main road connecting Bridgetown and the southern sections of these two parishes; Highway 3 goes to the northern sections. Roads are more crooked and confusing between these two highways than anywhere else on the island. Bring a good map.

Turn north off Highway 4 at Salters and you'll find **St. George's Parish Church,** which has some very interesting 17th-century furnishings. Continue on to **Gun Hill,** where you'll see the Gun Hill Signal Station and the inspiring Lion monument, one of the Barbados National Trust properties. North of Gun Hill on Highway 3, a southerly turn near Horse Hill will take you to **Cotton Tower,** another Barbados National Trust property, where you'll have a fine view of the **Scotland District** and the **East Coast Road.**

Francia Plantation near Gun Hill Signal Station in St. George, recently opened to the public, is an operating plantation that grows sugarcane and other crops. Here are unusual French architecture, a crystal chandelier in the panelled entrance hall, and other antiques. Open Monday to Friday 10 A.M.–4 P.M.; $3 admission.

This is where your map will come in handy. Side roads off both Highways 3 and 3B lead to the famous **Villa Nova,** a magnificently restored stately home, once owned by the late Earl of Avon, Sir Anthony Eden. The villa is one of

Barbados's great attractions for those with an interest in 17th- and 18th-century colonial society.

If you continue south, you'll rejoin Highway 3B, which will take you east to **St. John Parish Church,** then on to the sensational view from Hackleton's Cliff: the entire east coast from Pico Tenerife in the north to Ragged Point in the southeast. Check your map again and follow the side road southeast to **Codrington College,** whose history and Oxonian architecture could easily be within Oxford itself; only the lush foliage and brilliant flowers give away the tropical setting.

ST. THOMAS, ST. JOSEPH, AND ST. ANDREW

These parishes are best reached via Highway 2 from Bridgetown or Highway 1A from Holetown. Both roads lead to **Harrison's Cave** in central St. Thomas. It's one of the most spectacular natural cave systems in the Caribbean, and one of the most exciting attractions on Barbados, with a 36-passenger tram running deep into huge subterranean caverns, pools, and waterfalls. From Harrison's Cave, continue north on Highway 2 to one of the island's finest garden attractions, **Flower Forest** in St. Joseph. Stop along the way for a walk through unspoiled woodland, at another Barbados National Trust property, **Welchman Hall Gully.**

Now, you'll be entering the wild, ocean-whipped **Scotland District** of St. Joseph and St. Andrew, so named for its similarity to the Highlands. Here the rich fields grow sweet peppers, potatoes, beans, and tomatoes. Further north on Highway 2 is **Haggatts,** headquarters of the Barbados Soil Conservation and Rural Development Scheme, initiated in 1957 to develop forestry and prevent soil erosion, a serious problem in this part of the island. Just beyond, the eastbound road to Coggins Hill runs through the village of **Chalky Mount,** actually in St. Joseph, where artisans work on potters' wheels to fashion the local yellowish clay into a variety of items for sale.

The East Coast Road offers some of the most magnificent seascapes on Barbados: great stretches of deserted, windswept beach pounded by the Atlantic. You'll probably want to stop first at **Barclay's Park** for rest and refreshments, and maybe a walk on the beach. In Cattlewash, the **Kingsley Club,** a small inn, is worth a stop for one of their good tropical drinks or an excellent Bajan lunch—their fish is some of the best on Barbados.

Keep bearing left on this sinuous road and you'll see the signs leading to Bathsheba and one of the highlights of any visit to Barbados, **Andromeda Gardens.** If you're seriously interested in tropical horticulture, particularly for the opportunity to photograph many rare and unusual species, you'll want to allow an hour or two to explore this beautiful private collection of trees, shrubs, flowering plants, and succulents, which sprawls across a rocky hill carved with streams, small waterfalls, pools, and cobblestone pathways overlooking the fishing village of Tent Bay.

A fitting end to this tour is the **Atlantis Hotel,** a popular seaside bar and restaurant for real Bajan food, including reasonably priced flying fish and Bajan-style chicken. But because this has become a favorite stop of the tour buses, the once simple, down-home ambience can become frayed.

EAST FROM SPEIGHTSTOWN

East of Speightstown, Highway 1 curves through cane fields as it rises into the Scotland District of St. Andrew. At **Farley Hill National Park,** with the ruins of a once-magnificent sugar plantation, you'll enjoy walking through the grounds for a stunning view of the Scotland District.

Just across the road is the **Barbados Wildlife Reserve,** a habitat for green monkeys, in which other animals, including deer and wallabies, roam free in a very small mahogany forest. Visitors are allowed, but must not disturb the wild-life.

A mile and a half farther on is the turnoff north to **Cherry Tree Hill,** with a panoramic view of the Atlantic Coast. Plan to bring good shoes if you want to climb to the summit—the hill is steep and covered with loose rocks.

Down the road is the 17th-century **St. Nicholas Abbey,** one of only three remaining Jacobean Great Houses in the Western Hemisphere. Interesting features of this restored house include the fireplaces in its upstairs rooms, and four chimneys—obviously the architect was not expecting Bar-bados's tropical climate to extend to the hills of the Scot-land District.

Further south, **Morgan Lewis Mill,** part of the Bar-bados National Trust, is the only major windmill on the island with its working parts still intact. Inside is an exhibi-tion of artifacts and machinery used when sugar was pro-cessed by windpower in Barbados.

Within a few minutes along what is now Highway 2, is **St. Andrews Church,** which survived the devastating hurri-canes of 1780 and 1831 and was partially rebuilt in 1846. The nearby village of **Belleplaine** is the last busy outpost before the East Coast Road.

If you still have your map with you, follow a side road west of Highway 2 to **Turner's Hall Woods,** a 45-acre pre-serve which re-creates the kind of primeval forest which covered Barbados when the English settled here in 1627.

A side road south goes to 1,115-foot **Mt. Hillaby,** the highest point on the island. A narrow, winding road from the village of Hillaby leads to the summit, with magnificent views of the entire southern half of the island. If you haven't already stopped at **Welchman Hall Gully** or **Harrison's Cave,** you'll reach them a little further south along High-way 2.

St. James and St. Peter

The scenic parishes of St. James and St. Peter are home to most of the island's luxurious resorts. The outstanding properties are **Glitter Bay** and the **Royal Pavilion,** connected by a half mile of beach and 27 acres of gardens. The once-famed **Sandy Lane** resort four miles north of Bridgetown has an excellent 18-hole championship course at Payne's Bay. Nearby **Heron Bay** is one of the lovely homes of Barbados regularly featured in the winter Open House Program, but not open to the public otherwise. The new **Sir Frank Hutson Sugar Machinery Museum** shows a collection of old machinery and sugar production equipment.

Porters House, across from Colony Club resort near Holetown, is a great house dating back to the 17th century, set at the end of a long avenue of mahogany trees. A private residence, it is occasionally included in the Open House tours.

Holetown, today a busy tourist hub, is where the first party of English explorers landed in 1625. The Holetown Monument here bears the wrong date of 1605, however. The impressive coral-stone **St. James Parish Church** was the first church built in Barbados by the settlers who arrived in 1627. The structure has been rebuilt according to the original style and is surrounded by lovely gardens.

North of Holetown is **Folkestone,** site of one of many forts which protected the west coast, and now the location of the **Folkestone Underwater Park** (see *Water Sports*). There is a small museum here, but the main attraction is the protected reef area offshore, with an underwater trail marked for snorkelers and scuba divers.

Speightstown, in St. Peter's parish, was once considered the capital of the western parishes because of its busy port. All the sugar produced in this part of Barbados was shipped from here, and because much of that business was done with the English port of Bristol, Speightstown was nicknamed Little Bristol. In the center of town are the ruins of two battlements, **Orange Fort** and **Denmark Fort.** Speightstown itself retains the colonial appearance of many of its buildings, but is a busy shopping area for residents and visitors to the sprawling Heywoods resort complex nearby.

Heywoods itself is an attraction. Its Beach Village craft market offers a variety of gifts and souvenirs, and there are four restaurants and four bars. This is a nice spot to spend several hours—have lunch and relax on the beach, where you'll find a variety of water sports available.

Visitors are welcome to stop in and look around most of the hotel and resort properties, especially if they're interested in obtaining information for a future visit. Bars and restaurants are open to the public, but although all beach land in Barbados is public, access through private resorts is not. Most resorts allow lunch and dinner guests to use their facilities, but you should check with the front desk about policy. There are many superb resorts in this area, including the five **Elegant Resorts of Barbados,** which are worth seeing just for their splendid grounds. Barbados has some of the most outstanding properties in the Caribbean—many of them sightseeing attractions in themselves, like the 27 acres of landscaped gardens, with more than 10,000 plants, that connects Glitter Bay and the Royal Pavilion.

St. Lucy

The northernmost parish lies beyond Highway 1, where it forks into Highways 1B and 1C. The northern route will take you to North Point and the **Animal Flower Cave,** beyond Archer's Bay. An interesting, craggy coastline dominates this part of the island.

Historic Barbados

The Barbados National Trust was formed in 1961 for the preservation of buildings of architectural and historic interest and areas of natural beauty. The Trust welcomes new members, both residents and visitors, who may join for a $5 initiation fee and an annual membership fee of $15. Information is available from the Barbados National Trust Headquarters, Ronald Tree House No. 2, Tenth Ave., Belleville, St. Michael, Barbados (426–2421).

TRUST PROPERTIES

The following Trust properties are open to the public year-round.

Welchman Hall Gully, St. Thomas. A dense, wooded ravine edged by high cliffs, Welchman Hall Gully shows Barbados as the first settlers found it in 1627, covered with lush tropical forests. One of few remaining forested areas on Barbados, richly overgrown with such exotic tropical flora as bamboo, clove, nutmeg, cocoa, coffee, citrus, coconut, and the bearded fig trees for which the island was named. Occasionally you can see once-common green monkeys running wild through this area. Off Highway 2 near Sturges; admission $2,

Morgan Lewis Mill, St. Andrew. Built by Dutch settlers from Brazil, who pioneered the cultivation and processing of sugar cane, Morgan Lewis is the only wind-powered sugar mill on Barbados with its wheelhouse and sails still in perfect working order. It was still in use as late as 1947. North of Highway 2; admission $1.

Cotton Tower, St. Joseph. This was one of a chain of signaling stations built in the early 19th century to link the northern and eastern parts of the island with military headquarters in Bridgetown. Messages relayed between the towers gave early warning of approaching enemy ships. This structure was restored by the Trust and offers visitors outstanding panoramic views of the rugged east coast. Southeast of Highway 3, near Bathsheba; admission $1.

Gun Hill Signalling Station, St. George. Another historic building dating back to 1820, restored by the Trust and opened in 1982, the station may have the most beautiful view on Barbados. From here visitors can see a spectacular panorama of the whole southern section of the island. Try to come in the early evening. Also on this site is the famous **Gun Hill Lion,** 10 feet tall and 16 feet long, a magnificent creation sculpted in 1868 by Capt. Henry Wilkinson of the Norfolk Regiment. The statue represents Great Britain, with a Biblical inscription in Latin beneath, reading: "He shall have dominion also from sea to sea, and from river to river unto the ends of the earth." South of Highway 3B, west of Market Hill; admission $2.

National Trust Headquarters, Belleville, St. Michael. Located near Government House at the corner of Pine Rd. and 10th Ave. in Belleville, this is Barbados's archetypal Victorian home. Acquired by the National Trust in 1984, it is now a museum of Victorian Barbados, furnished with some of the island's finest furniture from the 1890s. The kitchen is particularly worth a look. The house is open Thursday afternoons in winter season 2–5 P.M., when hostesses dressed in Victorian costume offer guided tours. Admission $2.

Sir Frank Hutson Sugar Machinery Museum, housed in an old boiling house in St. James, shows original sugar processing machinery of yesteryear. The Portvale Sugar Factory next door is an example of a modern operating sugar processing plant.

THE GREAT HOUSES

Each Wednesday afternoon from mid-January to April the National Trust conducts its Open House program, with guided tours of stately homes and gardens. The $4 admission includes a drink. Some of the homes included in the program are new, striking examples of modern architecture in the tropics, but most are historic sites, some not normally open to the public. The most famous in this category are:

Sunbury House and Museum, St. Philip. Located on lovely grounds shaded by towering trees, this is the main house of a plantation dating to the 1660s. Recently restored by present owners, Mr and Mrs Keith Melville, it contains a private museum of antique furniture and household articles, as well as artifacts and vehicles from the turn of the century. Nearby is the **Chapel Plantation Coral Stone Quarry,** which until 20 years ago provided most of the hand-cut stone for building on Barbados. Also close by is the **St. Philip Parish Church,** whose churchyard has many huge kapok trees, and the vault of the family of Samuel Lord Hall (Sam Lord). Open year round.

Villa Nova, St. John. This is considered the best example of a 19th-century plantation house on Barbados, set in a spectacular six-acre garden on high ground, with outstanding views of St. John Parish. Built in 1835 by Edmund Haynes, whose family owned many island plantations, it was bought in 1965 by the late Sir Anthony Eden, Lord Avon, former Prime Minister of England. He wintered there for six years with his wife, and entertained many members of royalty, including Queen Elizabeth II and the Duke of Edinburgh. The present owners, Mr and Mrs Ernest Hunte, have restored the house with many antiques made from local mahogany. Open year-round.

Ilaro Court, Two Mile Hill, St. Michael. This extravagant house built of coral stone was designed in 1919 by Lady Gilbert Carter, the American wife of Sir Gilbert Carter, Governor of Barbados from 1904–1911. It is the official residence of the Prime Minister of Barbados, although the current Prime Minister Rt. Hon. E.W. Barrow does not live there. The house is unusual, combining several architectural styles: garden courtyard, ionic columns of carved stone coral, and an enclosed swimming pool—all set in a beautiful garden dominated by mahogany trees, and containing such exotic trees as teak, poinciana, ylang-ylang and Travelers' palm. Open only to special tours.

St. Nicholas Abbey, St. Peter. Built in 1650, just 25 years after the settlement of the island, and almost in its original condition, this is not only the most important historic house in Barbados, but also one of the oldest houses in the English-speaking Western Hemisphere. It is not an abbey, in the monastic sense. Its fine collection of English and Barbadian antiques includes an 1810 Coalport dinner service and a collection of early Wedgwood portrait medallions. Open year-round.

Drax Hall, St. George. Still in the hands of the Drax family, this great house dates from the 17th century. Its early Jacobean design, featuring archways carved in mastic wood no longer found on the island, is its most unusual feature. Open to public only for special tours.

OTHER ATTRACTIONS

Barbados Museum, the Garrison, St. Michael. The museum is located a mile southeast of Bridgetown in the old British Military Prison, built in 1835. It comprises several galleries of Indian artifacts, many West Indian prints dating back to the 17th century, some remnants of the early days of the sugar industry, and a comprehensive display of Barbados's history through post-slavery years. There are exhibits on antique maps and the flora and fauna of Barbados, and a library of West Indian art, where exhibitions are held regularly. Open Monday through Saturday, 9:00 A.M.–6:00 P.M.; admission $2.

Barbados Military Cemetery, St. Michael. Neglected for centuries, the cemetery has recently been cleaned and its gravestones restored; it is now a National Historic site. Many of the tombstones date back centuries, and bear inscriptions indicating the hazards, such as smallpox and yellow fever, which plagued early residents of the island. Free.

Codrington College, St. John. This magnificent structure, which resembles some of the colleges of Oxford, was originally the plantation home of Christopher Codrington, who in 1698, at the age of 30, became Governor General of the Leeward Islands. At his death in 1710 the College was established under his will. It opened in 1745 as a seminary for missionaries and medical aides, and was for a long time the oldest seminary in the Western Hemisphere. In 1875 it was affiliated with the University of Durham; since 1965 it has been part of the University of the West Indies. Its Oxonian quadrangle is one outstanding attraction, but the College Chapel is even more magnificent. Massive mahogany sanctuary rails and gates; the altar with pillars of cordia, lignum vitae, and ebony; brass chandeliers; and a stained-glass mosaic of the Good Shepherd are a few of its treasures. Equally impressive is the cabbage-palm drive leading up to the main house. Free.

Farley Hill National Park, St. Peter. The ruins of this once-opulent 19th-century plantation house and the spectacular view of the Scotland District and east coast make this a photographer's delight. Between 1856 and 1887, when the rambling manor house was the home of Sir Graham Briggs, a kind of West Indian Gatsby lifestyle of lavish parties and high living brought a stream of wealthy Europeans to this hilltop plantation. Unfortunately, the house was destroyed by fire, and its grand furnishing and decor lost. The gardens are now overgrown with a fine collection of trees, many of them planted by visiting dignitaries decades ago. Open daily 7 A.M.–6 P.M.; admission $1.

Cherry Tree Hill, St. Andrew. North of Highway 2 near the historic Morgan Lewis Sugar Mill, this is another of Barbados's great sightseeing stops: an avenue of towering mahogany trees leading to a fine view of the Scotland District from a point about 850 feet above sea level. Wear sturdy shoes—it's a steep walk from Morgan Lewis Mill. Occasionally you can see wild green monkeys scampering through the forest here.

Sam Lord's Castle, St. Philip. This superb mansion, built in 1820 by a resident rogue named Samuel Hall Lord, is now the centerpiece of a 256-room Marriott resort. The modern, luxurious hotel facilities have been isolated, on first view, from the fine old house, thanks to planning by Marriott, and the testimony to 19th-century opulence serves as both the main building and showpiece of the property, and as an historic attraction for visitors. Sam Lord was a Barbadian planter with a ruthless reputation for getting exactly what—and whom—he wanted. But the local legend of his wrecking practices—luring ships onto the reef with false lights, then plundering the wrecks—is only folklore.

The "castle" features a magnificent interior highlighted by carved mahogany columns, outlandish plaster ceilings, and an impressive collection of antique furnishings and art. The house is remarkably well-preserved, and its surrounding gardens carefully cultivated.

Christ Church Parish Church/Chase Vault, Christ Church. Overlooking the fishing community of Oistins, this is the fifth structure erected since the town was settled; the previous churches were destroyed by flood, hurricane or fire over the centuries. This site is legendary for the famous Chase Vault mystery dating back to the early 19th century. The vault, belonging to the Chase family, is in the churchyard, and when opened in 1812 for the burial of Colonel Thomas Chase, the heavy lead coffins within were found scattered in disarray. This incident occurred again in 1816 and 1817. Two years later, the Governor of Barbados witnessed the opening of the vault, and finding everything in order, affixed his seal in cement on the vault wall. But in 1820, disturbances started over again, and witnesses to the opening of the tomb found the coffins strewn about—but the seal unbroken. The family coffins were removed and buried separately in the churchyard. The mystery has never been solved.

South Point Lighthouse, Christ Church. Made entirely of cast iron in England, it was erected as part of the Great Exhibition of 1851 in London. Later that year, it was disassembled and shipped in sections to Barbados. It opened in April 1852.

Oistins, Christ Church. In this fishing community, the Charter of Barbados was signed in 1652, giving England dominion over the island. Today it is a busy fishing port, with an active open-air market which comes to life in late afternoon when the boats return. It is also the site of the Oistins Fish Festival each April.

Holetown, St. James. A monument with the wrong date commemorates the 1627 landing of the first Barbadians on the ship *Olive Blossom*. The town was so named because it reminded sailors of Limehouse Hole on the River Thames. The Holetown Festival celebrates that historic event each February.

Speightstown, St. Peter. This quaint seaside town was once a busy sugar port guarded by several military forts, and known as "Little Bristol." In recent years, attention has been paid to cleaning up the town and restoring the charming Colonial architecture of its buildings, while keeping pace with the modern tourism industry; branches of duty-free shops and supermarkets are recent additions.

CHURCHES

Every parish in Barbados has an Episcopal house of worship, most of them dating back centuries, while other smaller churches dot the landscape in varying architectural styles. In addition to Christ Church Parish Church, already mentioned, here are the more historic and architecturally interesting ones worth finding.

St. James Parish Church, St. James; off Highway 1. This is one of the four oldest remaining churches in Barbados. Originally built between 1627 and 1629, it has been carefully and elegantly restored in the past decade. The original stone structure lasted 200 years, but began to deteriorate badly around 1875. Some cosmetic work held the church together until serious restoration began in 1984. The magnificent stone building, set in lovely gardens, is a source of pride to the people of the parish.

St. Patrick's Cathedral, Bridgetown. The original church was built in 1840 and destroyed by fire in 1897. The present structure, rebuilt from funds donated by the government and a group of Protestant, Jewish, and Catholic benefactors, was opened on St. Patrick's Day 1899.

St. John Parish Church, St. John; at the end of Highway 3B, above Gall Hill. This beautiful old church overlooks the rugged east from an 800-foot cliff. Over 150 years old, it is a fine example of Barbadian Anglican Church architecture. In the graveyard is the ornate tomb of Ferdinando Paleologus, a descendant of Constantine the Great, the last Greek emperor, who was dethroned by the Turks at the fall of Constantinople.

St. George Parish Church, St. George; on a side road to Charles Rowe Bridge, north of Highway 4. This was one of only four parish churches which survived the devastating hurricane of 1831. Its outstanding feature is its magnificent altar painting, "The Resurrection," by Benjamin West, the first American president of the Royal Academy. There are some fine pieces of sculpture, including works by the creator of the statue of Lord Nelson in Bridgetown's Trafalgar Square, Richard Westmacott.

GARDENS, SCENIC POINTS, AND OTHER SIGHTSEEING ATTRACTIONS

Mount Gay Distillery, St. Lucy; south of Highway 1C in Fairfield. The distillery has been fully operational since the early 1800s, and produces 500,000 gallons of superior Barbados rum each year. Open Monday through Friday, 8 A.M. –4 P.M.; special tours Wednesdays.

Barbados Wildlife Reserve, St. Peter; across from Farley Hill National Park, north of Highway 1. This is an unusual and delightful natural park where the animals roam free and humans are confined to cobblestone walks. The beautiful, well-tended acres are home to a sizeable population of green monkeys, brought over from Senegal and the Gambia 350 years ago. This is a lovely, tranquil place to watch deer, hares, raccoons, wallabies, land tortoises, a variety of birds, small lizards, and a half dozen caimans (cousins of crocodiles). More animals are added each season. Open daily 9 A.M.–5 P.M.; admission $8 adults, $4 children.

East Coast Road, St. Andrew/St. Joseph. This coastal highway, opened by Queen Elizabeth II in 1966, follows an old railway route, passes spectacular scenes of the surf-pounded Atlantic coast with its fine, deserted beaches. It runs between Belleplaine and Bathsheba and ends with a view of Tent Bay.

Barclay's Park, St. Andrew. This 50-acre wilderness coastal park at the northern end of the East Coast Road was donated by Barclay's Bank to commemorate the Independence of Barbados in 1966. It's a beautiful beach, but dangerous currents beyond make it unsafe for anyone but very strong and cautious swimmers.

Chalky Mount Potteries, St. Andrew; off Highway 2, on the road to Coggins Hill. In the tiny village of Chalky Mount, 571 feet above St. Andrew, local potters work in small wooden houses, using treadle-run potters' wheels to fashion many interesting items from the yellowish clay of the area. Long ago, the Arawaks produced similar clay goods in Barbados. For a small fee, the potters will demonstrate their craft—and, of course, you're welcome to purchase anything that appeals to you.

Andromeda Gardens, St. Joseph. One of the show-places of the Caribbean, this magnificent estate was established in 1954 by the late Iris Bannochie and her husband John and is now under the auspices of the National Trust. It includes well over 200 species of tropical trees, plants, flowers, and flowering shrubs, planted amidst huge boulders, terraces, and pools. In this part of Barbados, different climates and soil conditions have allowed the owners to cultivate an incredible variety of plant life year-round. This is a horticulturist's and photographer's Eden, and serious botanists will want to spend several hours making a self-guided tour of the grounds. Some of the more startling attractions are the magnificent banyan tree (also known as bearded fig) and other trees that formed part of the primeval forest that covered Barbados; more than 100 varieties of hibiscus; a wide range of cacti, bromeliads, and succulents; and many species of orchids. Plants have been introduced to the garden from many Caribbean and other tropical countries. In return, the Bannochies sent specimens to such famous gardens abroad as the Royal Botanic Garden at Kew in England. Open 8 A.M.–dusk; admission $2 adults, $1 children.

Turner's Hall Woods, St. Andrew; North of Mt. Hillaby and west of Highway 2. This 45-acre preserve contains one of few remaining examples of primeval forest as settlers would have found it in 1627. Many vine-covered trees tower over this area, including locust, mastic, Spanish oak, "jack-in-the-box," kapok, cabbage palm, and mahogany. A beautiful natural place, where you can see a small boiling spring and, occasionally, wild green monkeys.

Mt. Hillaby, St. Andrew; west of Highway 2 near Baxters. This is the pinnacle of Barbados at 1,115 feet. A narrow, winding road leads almost to the summit from the village of Hillaby, rewarding the driver with extraordinary views of both coasts of the island.

Flower Forest, St. Joseph. Rising 850 feet above sea level, this lovely 50-acre site, once known as Richmond Plantation, has been developed into a sprawling flower garden beneath a variety of tropical fruit trees and banana groves. In addition to glorious flora, there are magnificent views of the Atlantic and Mt. Hillaby, the ruins of the sugar-boiling house and artifacts of the sugar industry; and a small, restored plantation house with a "Best of Barbados" gift shop and snack bar. Upon arrival, visitors are handed a leaflet suggesting the best routes for a self-guided tour of the forest's eight sections. Open daily, 9 A.M. until dusk;

admission $3. For special tours or information, call 433–8152.

Harrison's Cave, St. Thomas. One of the most striking natural attractions of Barbados, south of Highway 2 near Welchman Hall Gully, this is one of the finest cave systems in the Caribbean. The caves were first mentioned by a Dr. Packard in a letter written in 1796—and then forgotten for almost 200 years. In 1970, Danish speleologist Ole Sorensen rediscovered the cave system and approached the Barbadian Government about developing the area into an attraction for visitors. Work began in 1974 and the caves were opened to the public in 1981. A mile-long, one-hour trip by tram takes visitors through a subterranean spectacle of stalactites, stalagmites, cascading streams, and such sights as the 150-foot-long Great Hall, the Explorers' Pool, Twin Falls, Mirror Lake, and the Rotunda Room, a 250-foot-long, 100-foot-high chamber whose surface glitters like crystal. Tours every hour from 9 A.M.–4 P.M.; admission $5. Reservations suggested. Call 432–4048 for information.

Crane Beach Hotel, St. Philip. The pink sand beach below this cliffside resort has been a favorite of residents and visitors for centuries. The Crane Beach Hotel, one of Barbados's most elegant resorts, was built as a country mansion in 1790 and became the island's first "resort" in 1867. The $2.50 admission is refundable when you drink or dine.

Animal Flower Cave, St. Lucy. The name of this site at the end of Highway 1B is deceptive, but the scenery is worth the trip. The "Cave" was once a collection of limestone tide pools in which hundreds of sea anemones flourished. You can still see some, but the name is a lot more exotic than the reality. Call ahead (439–8797); the cave is closed on days when the sea is stormy. And bring a picnic basket. Open daily 9 A.M.–5 P.M.; admission $1.

Sports

Barbados is a perfect destination for those with a lot of energy to burn, especially those whose passion for sports spreads over land and sea. Barbadians' love of sports spans all seasons. From an almost universal obsession with cricket to an impetuous tendency to create new diversions suited to their countryside, like road rallies and cross-country cycling races, the people of this island love the outdoors and welcome visitors who want to participate.

ON DRY LAND

Cricket sometimes seems to be more of a religion than a sport, and from June to January radios broadcast little else. During the past 15 years, West Indies teams have dominated world play and Barbadian players have been in the spotlight. Barbados has won the West Indian Cricket Championship more times than any other Caribbean country and has been home to some fine cricketers, including Sir

Garfield Sobers, arguably the greatest of all time. Call 427–7415 for information.

The local **rugby** club, the Barbados Rugby Football Association, hosts overseas teams for matches several times each year. Their clubhouse and watering hole is located at the Garrison Savannah (436–6883). **Soccer,** known as football here, also has many avid supporters, as well as many leagues and competitions. Call 424–4413 for information.

Golf enthusiasts will find three courses under the aegis of the Barbados Golf Association, with a fourth scheduled to open for play by the beginning of 1991 at the Royal Westmoreland Golf and Country Club. The first Barbados Open Golf Championship will be held here. The Sandy Lane Golf Club (432–1145) has an 18-hole resort course constructed on the site of an old sugar-cane plantation. Splendid views of the Caribbean to the west and the Barbados countryside to the east make this a very attractive course. An old plantation-style club house offers bar and snack facilities, and the pro shop carries a full line of golf equipment and accessories. A resident pro and two assistants are available year-round, with special staff on hand from December through March. To play on this course, visitors must be guests at Sandy Lane or buy temporary membership, ($150 per week for individuals, $250 families). Green fees average between $25 and $30 for 18 holes; caddies, $13 for 18 holes; club rentals, $13 for 18 holes.

Both Rockley Resort in Christ Church (427–5890) and Heywoods in St. Peter (422–4900) have 9-hole courses which can be played as 18 holes, and both require players to use carts. Rockley's greens fees are $15 for 18 holes, $5 for 9 holes; Heywoods are $24 for 18 holes, $12 for 9 holes. Club rentals for both run $6–$7.50, carts (pull) $5 for 18 holes.

Tennis, often called lawn tennis here (not always correctly), is very popular, and there are too many hotel and resort courts to list. Resort guests may usually use courts free, with a small charge for racquet and ball rental. Your hotel activities desk can supply information. A recent count listed 29 resorts and apartment properties with at least one tennis court.

Squash courts are available at Heywoods, the Divi St. James Beach Resort, Barbados Squash Club (Marine House, Hastings, 427–7913), Rockley Resort Hotel, Casuarina Beach Club and Sea Breeze on the south coast. Cost is between $4 and $8 for 45 minutes on the courts.

Equestrian sports have long been among the island's popular diversions. The Barbados Turf Club (426–3980) has two racing seasons each year: January through May and July through October. Spectators gather en masse at Garrison Savannah on Saturday afternoons, most of them smartly dressed, garden-party style. Entrance fee to the grandstand is $2.50.

The British Army introduced **polo** to Barbados in the early 20th century. The Barbados Polo Club at Holders Hill, St. James (432–1802), hosts matches some Wednesdays, Saturdays, or Sundays during the September–March season. When visiting teams are here from England or the U.S., this is the place to see and be seen. Admission to the clubhouse is $2.50 and visitors are welcome.

Horseback riding averages $18–$26 per hour, including round-trip transportation from your hotel. All levels of riders can be accommodated, and Barbados currently has five small stables:

Valley Hill Stables, Christ Church (423–0033), offers rides through the hills of Christ Church Valley, through cane fields offering good views of this part of the island which some claim resembles the English countryside. English or Western saddle.

Ye Old Congo Road Stables, St. Philip (423–6180), takes riders through the grounds of old sugar plantations in the heart of St. Philip. English or Western saddle.

Country Corral Riding Stables, Taitts Plantation, St. James (422–2401), is the closest to the breathtaking views of the highland Scotland District. Riders cross countryside on the edge of St. Andrew parish, through cattle ranches at 900 feet—superb views of the entire island, and a memorable experience. Western saddle.

Brighton Stables, St. James (425–9381), is the outfit for those who'd like to ride along a tropical beach, and is the closest stable to the west-coast hotels.

Cycling buffs can rent bicycles for between $5 and $10 per day at Rent a Bike, located at Heywoods Resort (422–5398), M.A. Williams (427–1043), Chris Reid Bike Rental (427–7347) and Concord Bike Rental (428–7141). All will require a deposit (credit card acceptable). The Barbados Cycling Club organizes road races around the island and track races at the National Stadium. For information on any planned events during your stay, call 424–4486.

The Outdoors Club of Barbados (436–5328) organizes **hiking** outings on Wednesdays and Sundays and occasionally other days, beginning around 7 A.M. These "safaris" start with a long nature hike through one of the island's scenic areas, with commentary on local history, flora, and fauna by a club member. Later, there may be a beach picnic, cricket match, or barbecue. A day's outing, including transportation to and from hotel and meals, costs $70.

From early February through May the Barbados National Trust sponsors a series of Sunday morning walks. Led by young Barbadians and members of the National Trust, the hikes are designed to give visitors an interesting look at the natural beauty of the island while learning something about history and culture. During each hike, a speaker gives a brief educational talk on what the group will see that day, and a different area of the island is covered each week. Each walk begins at 6 A.M., covers about five miles, and takes about three hours. Transportation to the departure point can be arranged by calling the National Trust at least 24 hours in advance at 426–2421.

Marathons and **cross-country running** entered Barbados's sporting scene in 1983 with the running of the island's first marathon from Grantley Adams Airport to Heywoods. Since then the event, called Run Barbados has grown to include a weekend of long-distance and 10-kilometer competitions held in early December. The 10-kilometer is held in and around Bridgetown on Saturday morning. The marathon covers 26 miles, from the airport along the south coast and up through St. James and St. Peter to Heywoods. Entry fee is $10 per competitor per event, and forms can be obtained from the Amateur Athletic Association of Barbados, Box 46, Bridgetown, or any Barbados Board of Tourism office. Entries must be in by mid-November. Other local competitions are held throughout the year. Sports pages of the daily newspaper will have details of current events.

An international running group, the Hash House Harriers, sponsors relaxed jogging weekly in different parts of the island, with socializing afterward. For information, call Barry Johnson, 437–0827.

SEA SPORTS AND AQUATIC ADVENTURES

Isolated geologically as well as geographically from its Windward Island neighbors, Barbados combines two dramatically different coastlines into a varied paradise for the ocean enthusiast. Easternmost of all the Caribbean islands, Barbados faces the powerful Atlantic Ocean on the east and the tranquil Caribbean to the west. The western parishes of St. James and St. Peter offer palm-lined stretches of turquoise Caribbean waters, inviting simple splashers and adventurous divers alike. The white and windswept Atlantic beaches near Bathsheba and Cattlewash have dangerous currents and undertows which can threaten even the strongest swimmers.

Barbados is a coral island surrounded by small barrier reefs, which begin about 500 yards offshore. Until recently, it was not known for its underwater attractions, but scuba diving and snorkeling are growing in popularity and attracting a new kind of visitor to the island. Barbados now has over a dozen diving and water-sports operations, including a 28-passenger submarine for underwater sightseeing excursions. Visitors can see the ocean on glass-bottom boats, jet-skis, pedal-boats, windsurfers, parasailing "chutes", Hobie cats, Sunfish, waterskis, and day-cruise boats which offer life-threatening doses of rum punch onboard.

If you've never tried any of these unusual-sounding

activities, don't be intimidated. Qualified instructors can show you, step by step, how to handle a jet-ski, a Windsurfer, or a small sailboat. A basic course in scuba diving will enable you to make a real open-water dive on a shallow reef by the end of your stay. Many hotels and resorts offer complimentary water-sports instruction.

However you decide to enjoy the Bajan coastline, find yourself a good supply of waterproof sunscreen and apply it liberally, even if you're going to be underwater. Remember that water does not screen the sun's rays, but intensifies them.

SCUBA DIVING

The marine life in the shallow, reef-protected waters from Christ Church north to St. Peter is not as abundant as in some Caribbean destinations, but there is still plenty to see. The inner, shallow reefs along the coast offer a fine primer on common Caribbean reef life and easy diving or snorkeling. Low outcroppings of brain, finger, staghorn, star, and plate corals combine with a variety of gorgonians, sponges, and colorful reef fish. Life is more dramatic on the deeper bars, with a jungle of sponges and sea fans, sea whips and other gorgonians, with huge crinoids, giant feather duster worms, schools of surgeonfish and grunts, big lizardfish, Spanish mackerel, arrow crabs, and curtains of creole wrasses and chromis, to name a few.

Most dive sites are located on the southwest and west coasts, which comprise a curious underwater topography. Here, sandy trenches and buttes rise from the ocean floor, with the first beginning between 1/4 and 1/3 mile offshore at a depth of 120 feet, rising to within 55 feet of the surface. This hill-and-dale formation continues until the "bars," as they are called locally, become too deep for diving at 130–150 feet, creating a series of double-sided drop-offs which are a wall-diver's dream. All but a few sites are drift dives because of a common 1–2 knot current running from the southeast, and all calculations are in the metric system, which may confuse U.S. divers. Visibility is predictably good between 75 and 100 feet, except when the occasional squall or nor'wester churns up the water.

In recent years, Barbados's main underwater attractions have been its wrecks, the largest and best known being the *Stavronikita,* a 356-foot Greek cargo ship which caught on fire in August 1976 and went adrift while en route from Ireland to Barbados. The ship was later purchased for $30,-000 by the Barbadian government. A group of local investors, including dive operators, pooled their talents to create an artificial reef with the ship rather than convert it to scrap metal. Using 200 lbs. of dynamite, and assisted by a U.S. Navy demolition crew, they sank the "Stav" in 130 feet of water off St. James beach in November 1978. Its hull has already attracted a substantial marine menagerie, including encrusting corals and sponges and reef fish.

Another popular site for divers and snorkelers lies in Carlisle Bay, in only 25 feet of water. The *Berwyn* is a World War I French tug, encrusted with corals and sponges since its sinking in 1919. The deck rises to within 10 feet of the surface, making this a very easy place to see a variety of fish and other marine life.

Carlisle Bay has two other wrecks, and local records indicate at least a dozen more undiscovered ships rest on its floor. The wooden hull of the *Marian Bell Wolfe* has lain under 40 feet of water since 1955, attracting schools of fish. The *Granny* lies in 45 feet, and only a part of her metal structure is still visible, but it has attracted a fascinating variety of marine life, including rays and the occasional moray eel. Carlisle Bay was the anchorage for dozens of 17th- and 18th-century ships, and quantities of bottles and other artifacts are recovered each year by enthusiastic divers and snorkelers.

By far the most famous sightseeing spot is the Barbados Marine Reserve, in Folkestone National Park, off St. James. This underwater park is protected by law, and visitors must not touch or remove anything. In a special recreational zone, snorkelers and divers can follow an underwater trail along Dotting's Reef, with many examples of marine life marked and identified by small plaques. There are two other areas, one for marine research only, and another for sailing, skiing, and other sports, away from the reef trail. Park headquarters are at Folkestone House, where a small museum, marine laboratory, and exhibit of photographs and artifacts is open Monday through Saturday for a small admission charge.

Diving in Barbados is monitored by the recently formed Eastern Caribbean Safe Diving Association, which works to make sure the island's 13 diving- and water-sports-related businesses adhere to safety standards. There is a recompression chamber on Barbados now, located in the compound of the Barbados Defense Force. Divers wishing to experience this side of Barbados should bring their C-cards; complete equipment rentals are available locally, but you'll save a substantial amount of money if you bring your own (except tank, back pack, and weights). Average price of a one-tank boat dive is $25–30 per person if you furnish your own equipment.

Novices can learn to dive on Barbados, but not all dive shops have trained, certified instructors, so you should call in advance to make arrangements. Short, introductory courses—called "resort courses"—take a day and cost about $75, including equipment and a shallow open-water dive upon course completion. **Willie's Watersports** at Hey-

woods, St. Peter (422–4900 or 424–1808), offers a variety
of water sports, including waterskiing, windsurfing, Sunfish
sailing, glass-bottom-boat trips, and snorkeling cruises on
the 41-foot yacht *Shady Lady*. **The Dive Shop Ltd.** (426–
9947 or 426–0890), in Aquatic Gap near the Grand Bay
Hotel, is the place to go for diving in Carlisle Bay and trips
to the southwest coast. They offer a full program of scuba
lessons, equipment rentals, and daily boat trips, as well as
other water sports. **Underwater Barbados** at Southwinds
Beach Resort in St. Lawrence Gap is another good operation with full-service dive shop and water sports on the
beach. **Les Wotton Scuba School & Watersports** at the
Coral Reef Club, St. James (422–3215/432–0833); **Dive
Barbados** at Sunset Crest Beach Resort, St. James (432–
6666) and Sandy Beach Hotel, Christ Church (428–9033);
Dive Boat Safari at the Barbados Hilton (427–4350) and
Village Watersports, Barbados Beach Village, St. James
(425–1440) are other diving and water-sports centers on
the west and south coasts. Diving is not advised on the east
coast of Barbados, due to rough seas and strong currents.

These water-sports operations also give instructions to
beginning snorkelers, and organize snorkeling trips for a
small fee, if you're not confident about donning tanks yet.
Many hotels offer free use of water-sports equipment to
guests (mask, fins, snorkels, waterskis, Sunfish), so you
should check with your hotel activities director for information.

WINDSURFING

This sport has grown tremendously in popularity during
the past few years, and Barbados is the ideal island for it.
In 1982, the Barbados Windsurfing Club was established in
Maxwell on the south coast; in 1983, Mistral, a leading
manufacturer of windsurfing equipment, held its world
championship here, and today, there is a **Club Mistral** at the

Barbados Windsurfing Club (428–9095). Top equipment—including 60 of the latest boards—and lessons are available. Board rental costs around $8–$15 per hour, with lessons about the same price. The Club has 15 rooms for rent, as well as a restaurant and bar.

Windsurfing is available at other hotels along the south and west coasts.

SURFING

Surfing is popular with the locals, who test their hang-ten skills both on the south coast and on the Atlantic side, which offers excellent surfing conditions from time to time. Local surfing championships are held in November. The water-sports concession at the Hilton rents fiberglass surfboards for about $7 per hour, with deposit.

SAILING AND CRUISING

Many of the water-sports concessions listed under *Diving* also rent jet-skis and various small sailboats, including Sunfish and Hobie-Cats, and will teach you how to handle the equipment. Sailing cruises on larger craft, for snorkeling/lunch cruises and circumnavigating the island, are available on *Shady Lady,* booked through Willie's Watersports; the catamaran *Tiami* (424–0172/428–8276); *Jolly Roger,* a pirate barquentine replica (432–7090); *Irish Mist* (435–6037) and the Mississippi riverboat *Bajan Queen* (436–2149). Prices are $25–$38 per person for a 3- to 5-hour trip including lunch, drinks, and use of snorkeling equipment. Evening dinner-and-dance cruises are also available at slightly higher prices.

DEEP-SEA FISHING

Judging from the quantity of fresh local fish like kingfish, tuna, and dolphin (the fish, not the mammal), appearing on local restaurant menus, it's obvious that fishing is good in outlying waters, but sport-fishing has not been developed as one of Barbados's main tourist attractions. For one thing, big fish such as blue marlin, white marlin, wahoo, and tuna run in deep water, and local captains will admit it can be a long run to find them. Four- to six-person charters, including drinks, bait, and tackle, cost about $350 per half-day or $700 for a full day. Contact the *Blue Jay* at 422–2098, or *Scotch 'n Soda* charters at 428–7308.

Parasailing

Hardly a sport, parasailing involves strapping on a parachute-like contraption and letting a speedboat tow you until you're gliding through the air. Called "para-gliding" here, it's a relatively new addition to Barbados's recreational offerings, and an operation called **Chute the Moon** (422–1357) offers 10-minute rides 200 feet above the west-coast beaches for $25. The operation is located at Holetown Beach, near the Barbados Pizza House in St. James.

Submarine rides

Nondivers and families rave about the daytime and nighttime dives aboard the 28-passenger *Atlantis II* submarine (436–8929). A two-mile ferry trip from the Careenage in Bridgetown takes you to the dive site, where you transfer to the sub, which comes alongside. On board the *Atlantis II,* air-conditioning, soft music, and a fish identification chart at your own porthole enhance the views of the subsea panoramas, including coral reefs and the wreck of the *Stavronikita.* Twelve dives daily, to a maximum of 150 feet; about $50 per person.

Yachting

Whether you're an avid yachtsman arriving on your own boat, or just looking for the company of kindred sea folks, you'll find a welcome from members of the **Barbados Yacht**

Club (427–1125) or the **Barbados Sailing and Cruising Club** at Gravesend Beach (Carlisle Bay, 426–4434). Visiting yachtsmen congregate in the Boatyard Restaurant and Bar on Carlisle Bay.

December each year marks the annual A.R.C. trans-Atlantic race from Las Palmas in the Canary Islands to Bridgetown. The 2,700-mile race takes almost three weeks and draws about 300 entries. If you're in Barbados around Christmastime, contact the clubs above for information— it's an exciting week when the yachts arrive, and plenty of post-race activities are planned.

Boxing Day (Dec. 26) brings the annual three-day **Mount Gay Regatta** for local sailing enthusiasts, and regattas are scheduled from time to time on other holidays. Details appear in the *Visitor* and local newspaper sports sections.

BEACHES

If you had the good fortune to arrange an aerial sightseeing tour of the island, you'd quickly see just how many lovely beaches Barbados has. The best lie on the west coast—in St. Michael, St. James, St. Peter, and St. Lucy—which is the leeward side for most of the year. All of them are public, even if the resorts fronting on them are not.

St. Michael's most popular beaches are the long stretch at the Hilton, the public area along Carlisle Bay, Browne's Beach beyond the Bay St. fish market, Paradise Beach Hotel, Brandon's, and Batt's Rock, an undeveloped stretch of beach north of Cunard Paradise Beach.

In St. James, the most magnificent stretches trim Payne's Bay and extend along most of the coast through Sandy Lane Bay into Holetown. The sister resorts of Glitter Bay and the Royal Pavilion, with more than half a mile of connecting beach, are upscale properties; you will want to bring along appropriate beach coverups.

Cobblers Cove resort in St. Peter's has a secluded, palm-lined cove, and Gibbs Bay and Mullins Bay have good open beach areas. The mile-long beach at Heywoods Resort is one of the finest in the Caribbean.

In contrast, beaches are wild and undeveloped on the rocky Atlantic Coast. North to south, you'll find breathtaking views at Morgan Lewis Beach, Long Pond, Tent Bay, and Barclay's Park, near Bathsheba on the East Coast Road. Plan to pack a picnic lunch if you head for the Atlantic Coast; outside of Cattlewash and Bathsheba there's very little to buy.

In St. John, a popular beach follows the coast at Bath, near Consett Bay. In St. Philip, the best stretch lies between Bottom Bay and the often-photographed beach near the Crane Hotel.

All along the south-coast parish of Christ Church you'll find good beaches, breezier than the western ones, but not surf-pounded like those on the Atlantic coast; and Christ Church's coastline probably has more funky beach bars and rum shops per square mile than any place in the Caribbean.

Warning: Especially on the Atlantic side be extremely cautious, as strong currents can create dangerous undertows. Only wading and splashing are suggested—never go in over your head.

Resorts

Barbados can advertise honestly that it has resorts and accommodations to suit every taste—unless you want a private island to yourself. With over 14,000 hotel and guest-house beds available, ranging from luxurious suites to informal bungalows, and another several hundred in rental villas and houses, you could enjoy a different holiday lifestyle every time you returned to this island—for years.

Christ Church has the greatest number of guest houses, small resorts, and rental cottages—as well as several fine larger hotels. Luxurious suites and villas are most numerous along the beaches of St. James and St. Peter. St. Michael has two fine new resorts, both with excellent beaches and convenient to Bridgetown.

Package tours frequently offer the best resort buys. Many varieties are available, from all-inclusive vacations, which include everything from drinks and meals to water sports, to scuba-diving packages and other sports-oriented

BARBADOS RESORTS

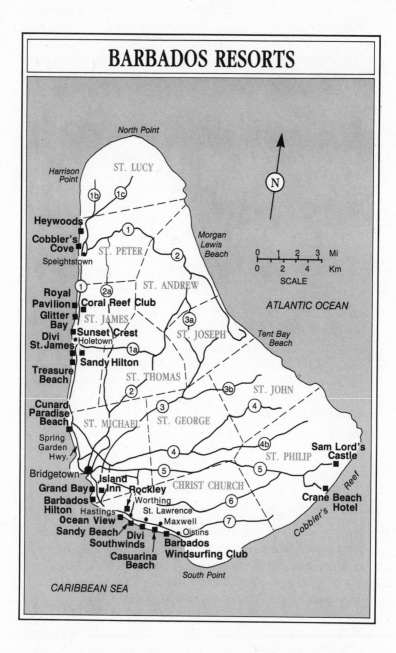

North Point

Harrison
Point

ST. LUCY

(1b) (1c)

Heywoods

**Cobbler's
Cove**

Speightstown

ST. PETER

(1)

(2)

Morgan
Lewis
Beach

ST. ANDREW

(2a)

**Royal
Pavilion**

Coral Reef Club

ST. JAMES

**Glitter
Bay**

Sunset Crest

Holetown

(3a)

ST. JOSEPH

Tent Bay
Beach

**Divi
St. James**

(1a)

Sandy Hilton

**Treasure
Beach**

ST. THOMAS

(2)

(3b)

ST. JOHN

**Cunard
Paradise
Beach**

ST. MICHAEL

(3)

ST. GEORGE

(4)

Spring
Garden
Hwy.

(4)

(4b)

ST. PHILIP

**Sam Lord's
Castle**

Bridgetown

**Island
Inn**

(5)

(5)

Grand Bay

Rockley

CHRIST CHURCH

Worthing

**Barbados
Hilton**

Hastings

St. Lawrence

(6)

**Crane Beach
Hotel**

Ocean View

Maxwell

Sandy Beach

**Divi
Southwinds**

Oistins

(7)

**Barbados
Windsurfing Club**

**Casuarina
Beach**

South Point

Cobbler's Reef

CARIBBEAN SEA

ATLANTIC OCEAN

0   1   2   3 Mi
0   2   4   Km
SCALE

N

deals. Another money-saving option is the MAP (Modified American Plan). By paying a supplement of $30–$55 per person daily, you can get breakfast and dinner included in the price of your stay, often with a dine-around option at a number of participating resorts with restaurants. Packages are sold through travel agents, who can tailor a holiday to match your special interests and tastes.

As mentioned earlier, most room rates are reduced by as much as 40% from May through November. Sharing a two- or three-bedroom villa, apartment or house with friends can be one of the best values of all. Not only will your room rate be reasonable, but you'll also be able to save on your dining expenses. All villa rentals include maid service; some include a cook.

If you decide on a "self-catering" vacation in a villa or house, you'll find it convenient to use Barbados's well-stocked supermarkets and fish and produce shops. Prices are shockingly high, however, since many food items must be imported. If a cook is included in your arrangement, she will do the shopping for you.

Note: All rates quoted below are for doubles, per day, in high season, meals not included.

RENTING A VILLA
OR LUXURY HOME

Barbados has its own local rental agencies, which have extensive listings and act as property managers year-round. This means if you have any problems while you're on the island, there will be someone to assist you—a definite advantage when you're hundreds of miles from home. They include:

Alleyne, Aguilar & Altman, "Rose Bank," Derricks, St. James, Barbados (432–0840). **Bajan Services,** Seascape

Cottage, Gibbs, St. Peter (422–2618). **Ronald Stoute & Sons Ltd.,** Sam Lord's Castle, St. Philip (432–6800). **Realtors Limited,** Riverside House, River Rd., St. Michael (426–5248).

One group of villas offers access to the facilities of the Cunard Paradise Beach Hotel at very reasonable rates. **Beyond the Blue** has two one-bedroom villas and one three-bedroom unit with maid service, beginning at $600 per week. Contact Willie Hassell, Black Rock, St. Michael (424–1808/1809).

In general, rental rates on villas and houses follow the pattern for other accommodations: summer rates are substantially lower. Even in winter season, however, rates can be as low as $800 per week for a villa that could be shared by two couples or four people. They can also be $3,000 or more for a luxury home in a private landscaped garden with complete staff.

Vacation apartments

Barbados has several hundred vacation apartments with spacious, fully equipped kitchens. You can obtain a brochure listing available rentals and their rates from the Barbados Board of Tourism's offices—most of these complexes are in Christ Church and St. James.

Divi Southwinds Beach Resort in St. Lawrence offers 166 fully air-conditioned units—regular guest rooms, studios, and one- and two-bedroom suites—all have kitchenette facilities. The resort is set in 20 lovely acres of tropical gardens on a half-mile of white sand beach, with three fresh-water swimming pools, two lighted tennis courts, and two excellent restaurants. Its location in St. Lawrence Gap makes it convenient walking distance to many shops, restaurants, and markets. One of the best attractions is Southwinds' complete scuba diving operation,

Underwater Barbados. $160–$250. For information: DIVI Hotels, 520 West State St., Ithaca, NY 14850. (800–367–DIVI or 607–277–3484).

Another Divi resort offering this dual-vacation option of rooms or suites in St. James is the **Divi St. James Beach Resort.** This lovely beachfront property has two fresh-water pools, a full range of complimentary water sports for guests (including exchange privileges with Southwinds for tennis and scuba diving), and its own fitness complex. Its alfresco Sand Dollar restaurant has excellent local entertainment several nights a week, and its All Night Long Piano Bar is open from 10 P.M. until very late. No children under 16 are permitted in winter season. $180. Same address and phone as Southwinds for information.

Long a favorite with regular visitors, the **Rockley Resort and Beach Club** in Worthing, Christ Church, is one of Barbados's most complete resorts, with 365 luxurious studios and one- and two-bedroom apartments, each with fully equipped electric kitchens and private patio. The resort includes a private beach club with water sports, seven swimming pools, five tennis courts, two air-conditioned squash courts, a 9-hole golf course, volleyball facilities, and a supermarket. For nightlife, you'll find a good restaurant, two bars, a disco, and a regular entertainment schedule during the week, highlighted by a Sunday Beach Party with steel band. The apartments are about one-half mile from the beach; there is a regular free shuttle service. Two-bedroom apartments $200; studios $100. Box 7835, Orlando, FL 32854. Call 800–223–9815 or 212–840–6636 for information.

The **Casuarina Beach Club** in St. Lawrence Gap faces out on a beautiful pine-lined beach on the quiet south coast. Each of the studio apartments has a kitchen, air-conditioning, phone, and a private balcony. There's a restaurant on the beach, if you don't feel like cooking, and for leisure time, there's tennis, squash, a 900-foot beach, and water sports. $110. For information, call 800–223–9815 or 212–840–6636.

Another bargain apartment complex is the **Sunset Crest Resort,** about seven miles north of Bridgetown in St. James. Apartments and villas of various sizes are clustered around a small "village" which includes a supermarket/deli, (open seven days a week), liquor store, bank, department store, and club house. Recreation facilities include six swimming pools, six tennis courts, a small golf course, and a beach club, as well as two restaurants and bars. $80–$110. For information, call 432–6666 or 800–223–1588.

In addition to these recommended spots, many hotels falling into the "elegant" or "deluxe" price range also offer suites with kitchenettes and living/dining areas.

SPECIAL RESORTS

An entire guide book could be written about the full-service resorts on Barbados. Here is a look at some of the outstanding ones.

On the distant Atlantic coast of St. Philip, Marriott's **Sam Lord's Castle** is popular not only for the restored mansion of the legendary rogue, but also for its fine 260-room resort, set in 72 tropical acres. The 19th-century castle is the showpiece of the resort, rising white and impressive above fountains and gardens which are a year-round floral festival. A huge fresh-water swimming pool, tennis courts, a full weekly program of entertainment, boutiques, and water sports are just part of the attraction of this secluded resort. The variety of dining options makes it exceptional: five restaurants! The Cobblers Reef is the formal gourmet restaurant, requiring jacket and tie and reservations, but the Sea Garden and the casual Wanderer are there for less formal dining. At the weekly Castle Dinner, featuring a formal banquet in the Castle, seven courses are served on an elegant long table; reservations in advance are a must. Bajan Fiesta and Pirate's Shipwreck barbecue nights draw visitors from other parts of the island. $180–$245. For information, call 800–228–9290 or 212–265–4040.

St. Philip's other special property is the island's oldest hotel, the **Crane Beach Hotel.** The main house is an 18th-century mansion which sits on a bluff overlooking 1,000 feet of pink-sand beach and a secluded coconut grove 60 feet below. Formerly a small, romantic resort with only 25 rooms, the Crane Beach will add 100 rooms for the 1990 season. A dramatic pool of Romanesque design has marble columns and decorative railings trimming the terrace edge. The restaurant offers candlelight dining and superb fresh seafood from nearby Cobblers Reef; at night floodlights enhance the spectacular view of the ocean. Non-hotel guests can spend a Sunday here for $35, which includes a popular Sunday Bajan buffet lunch. Tea is served daily, 3–6 P.M. Doubles $225, suites $300–$450. Prices of new accommodations to be announced. Call 800–223–6510 for information.

Back on the south coast in Christ Church, just west of Oistins, is the informal **Barbados Windsurfing Club Hotel,** which for the past four years has been the site of the Club Mistral, one of the world's leading windsurfing schools. The resort has only 15 rooms in a beachfront setting, but its bar is a popular gathering place, especially for water-sports buffs. $70–$120. Information: 428–9095/7277.

Every room is a motel-like suite at the **Sandy Beach,** a Best Western resort. In addition to kitchen facilities and air-conditioning, each of the 88 units has satellite TV available at an extra $5 per day, for the traveler who can't exist without news. There are 38 one-bedroom and 50 two-bedroom suites, and complimentary water sports on a fine beach for all guests. The resort is surrounded by two acres of tropical garden, close to shops and entertainment in the Worthing area of Christ Church. Its Green House restaurant is popular for Bajan and Continental specialties, and the beachfront Sand Bar has a regular schedule of live local entertainment. $175–$300. For information, call the Best Western Reservations Office in your area or 800–528–1234.

Just over a mile south of Bridgetown, the Aquatic Gap section of St. Michael has three noteworthy hotels. Charming for its purely Bajan ambience and brilliant bougainvillea gardens, the 24-room **Island Inn** is a short walk from Gravesend Beach and Carlisle Bay. Its low rates and friendly staff make this a special find for travelers who like local flavor. The Inn's Barracks restaurant has been completely refurbished. The Dive Shop Ltd. offers water sports nearby. Doubles $50; singles $37. For information, call 436–6393 or write directly to the Island Inn at Aquatic Gap, Garrison St., St. Michael, Barbados.

A clublike feeling characterizes the **Ocean View** on Hastings Road in Hastings, where 40 rooms cling to the south coast. The lovingly tended grande dame is filled with the owner's antiques, seven crystal chandeliers, and masses of floral arrangements. The cap to any stay is an invitation to dinner in the private Crystal Room. Everyday dining offers a mixture of West Indian and Continental cuisines.

Entertainment on Thursday and Friday evenings in season. Suites $110, doubles $70–$85, singles $50–$65. For information, 427–7821 or 427–7823.

The 14-acre **Barbados Hilton** has recently upgraded its 185 rooms with bright tropical decor, mini-bars, TV, phones, radio, and air-conditioning. A shopping arcade with duty-free shops greets guests at the entrance. Within are four lighted tennis courts, a huge beach (you can even surf here at certain times of the year) and free water sports (scuba extra) for all guests. The two restaurants and bars have also been upgraded, but the highlight at the Hilton after dark is its weekly entertainment program (see *Nightlife*). Golfers and horseback riders can be accommodated nearby too. $175–$210. For information, call Hilton International Reservations, 800–445–8667.

The showpiece of Carlisle Bay is the **Grand Barbados Beach Resort,** a former Holiday Inn transformed into a spectacular resort. Each of the 133 rooms has been stripped and redecorated in exceptional tropical decor, with two double beds, air-conditioning, radio, and telephone. The sixth and seventh floors of the main building are the Executive Club floors, with a hospitality suite for businessmen staffed by a full-time receptionist who can arrange complete secretarial services. Those rooms are also equipped with mini-bars and bathroom phones. An exercise room is nearby. Standard and luxury suites on the pier section include living-room areas and wet bars. One hundred guest rooms have ocean views; all have mini-bars, hairdriers, and TV, with eight-channel satellite reception at no extra charge.

The Grand Barbados has an attractive location on a fine section of Carlisle Bay. Complimentary water sports include certified Mistral windsurfing school, Sunfish sailing, snorkeling, glass-bottom-boat rides, and pool instruction on scuba. The hotel also has its own 35' trimaran, *Free Spirit*, which can be rented for lunch and cocktail cruises.

The two restaurants of the Grand Barbados are the Golden Shell and the Schooner. The elegant Golden Shell, behind stained-glass windows, seats 76 diners in a formal, romantic atmosphere. The Schooner, overlooking the Caribbean at the end of the resort's 260-foot pier, offers daily seafood buffet lunch and dinner specials.

Suites $550, standard rooms over $200; MAP dine-around $60. For information: International Travel and Resorts, 4 Park Ave., New York, NY 10016 (800–223–9815).

The **Cunard Paradise Beach Hotel & Club** is a beach-front property in Black Rock, at the northern edge of St. Michael. Just over two miles from Bridgetown, this 12-acre resort is working hard to become another popular water-sports mecca, offering guests complimentary waterskiing, snorkeling, windsurfing, tennis, Sunfish sailing, two fresh-water pools, and a beach. Cars are prohibited on the grounds, and guests who don't care to walk are transported by tram.

The resort features three beachfront restaurants and a busy entertainment program. Each of the 180 rooms and suites was redecorated recently. Doubles $200–$220. For information, 800–528–6273 or 800–223–0888.

The 380-acre **Sandy Lane Hotel and Golf Club** has drawn the rich and famous to its beautiful St. James beach-front location. Among its attractions are an 18-hole championship golf course, complimentary tennis, and a mammoth swimming pool. Its 112 double rooms and suites rank among the most expensive accommodations in the Caribbean; whether they're worth the rates is debatable, as service is often indifferent. But because the enclave has been on the itinerary of so many celebrities and dignitaries, its reputation prevails, and it is now one of five members of the **Elegant Resorts of Barbados** association. Sprawling, plantation-like grounds reflect its origins as a sugar estate. Water sports are available on the beach; the three restaurants include the pricey and formal Sandy Bay, with regular entertainment. Doubles $460–$1,100 MAP, in season. Information: 800–223–5672 or 800–223–1230.

WEST COAST RESORTS

Just south of Sandy Lane in Payne's Bay is the delightful **Treasure Beach Resort,** with 24 ocean-view suites in a beautiful garden setting. Service is excellent; the staff here actually outnumber the guests. The resort's restaurant is a Gold Award winner in Barbados—the outstanding hotel restaurant on the island—and it attracts a lot of non-resident diners to the property, particularly for the weekly Caribbean Buffet. Swimming pool and water sports for guests and an intimate ambience make this a special place. Closed September through mid-October. Doubles $210–$290, MAP supplement $50 per person. For information, contact Robert Reid Associates, 800–223–6510 or 432–1346.

North of Holetown is the **Coral Reef Club,** located on 12 acres of beachfront gardens. In this 30-year-old resort you'll find 75 rooms arranged in suites and cottages, each with a patio or balcony where room-service breakfast is available every morning. The resort's beach is considered one of the finest on the St. James coast, and guests can enjoy waterskiing, windsurfing, parasailing offshore, or snorkeling and scuba lessons in the fresh-water pool. Two tennis courts complete the recreation facilities for sports lovers.

The Coral Reef Club retains a relaxed English elegance and excellent service. Four-star dining in the hotel's restaurants is an expected part of guests' vacations. No children under 12 in winter season. Doubles $300–$435, including three meals daily. Information: Ralph Locke Associates (800–223–1108).

Glitter Bay Resort is worth a visit just to enjoy the gardens spread over the 27 acres that link the resort with the Royal Pavilion. The main building resembles a plantation manor house, and each of the 84 rooms in the white stucco four-story buildings offers a feeling of privacy. The resort has been completely renovated for 1989–1990.

The property was originally purchased around 1900 by a prominent Barbadian businessman as his private beachfront estate. In the 1930s, Sir Edward Cunard, of the English shipping family, bought the estate, built the main Great House, began the elaborate landscaping of the grounds, and completed this tropical Eden with a beach house similar to the Cunard family palazzo in Venice. Cunard hosted famous parties in honor of visiting aristocrats and celebrities, and Glitter Bay became synonymous with grandeur.

The beach house has just reopened and often features well-known names on the international circuit. The Great House is now the elegant reception area and private guests' lounge, offering complimentary afternoon tea and evening cocktails for all guests.

For recreation, guests can enjoy two free-form freshwater pools, lighted tennis courts, and complimentary water sports (sailing, windsurfing, snorkeling, and waterskiing) on a half-mile stretch of beach that reaches to the Royal Pavilion. (Guests of both resorts have exchange privileges.) Penthouse $1,100, one-bedroom suites $400, doubles $310. For information, contact Robert Reid Associates at 800–223–6510.

The **Royal Pavillion** shares with Glitter Bay the 27 acres of manicured gardens (with some 10,000 plants) and a half-mile of beach. The rooms here are 72 oceanfront suites, each with private balcony, and three-bedroom villas. Guests can sign for anything from diving to dining. The pampered Simese cats who roam the property, "Rum" and "Coke," are under the personal protection of the owner. Suites $250 in season, villas $450 (for a party of six), MAP

$50 additional. Information from Robert Reid Associates, 800–223–6510.

Just south of Speightstown in St. Peter is **Cobblers Cove**. There's a lot that's attractive about this 38-room hotel, but its palm-lined cove and quiet beach are at the top of the list. An atmosphere of romance permeates the place.

Each luxurious one-bedroom suite is done in bright tropical decor, with a well-stocked kitchenette, and the profusion of "little, extra touches"—bathroom baskets overflowing with fine English soaps; huge, plush towels; fresh flowers everywhere—is what you always hope to find on check-in, but seldom do today. The staff is as loyal as the repeat clientele they service, and after a week here you'll feel like you've had a personal maid/helper who has been in the family for years. The service and intimacy of Cobblers Cove are truly outstanding. The suites are in fresh, white-washed buildings by the beach, surrounded by flowering shrubs and gardens of colorful tropical plants. The open-air restaurant has a reputation for an outstanding five-course table d'hôte, and the beach bar offers a staggering variety of imaginative—and deadly—rum creations.

The main building looks like a pastel castle and offers guests a private, elegant sitting room and quiet bar beyond. Every morning, the resort offers a mini-bus sightseeing service to Bridgetown (saving you a $35 cab trip) and the property is within walking distance of quaint Speightstown for shopping or sightseeing. There's a good fresh-water pool by the beach, and tennis and golf can be arranged nearby. Doubles $400–$800 MAP, in season. Exchange-dining with other hotels for MAP guests. Information through Robert Reid Associates (800–223–6510).

Heywoods, owned by the Barbados government, occupies 30 beachfront acres in the northern part of St. Peter, about 15 miles from Bridgetown. A world of its own, Heywoods is a good site for meetings and conventions, with four restaurants, four bars, a disco, many water sports, squash and tennis, three pools, and a 9-hole golf course. Most guests never realize there are 306 rooms here, they're distributed so subtly among seven buildings.

Each of the interconnecting and individually named buildings offers a choice of rooms, or suites with kitchenettes; TV is available for an extra fee. You can choose the 32-room Antillean, with a West Indian folk-theme decor; the 58-room Sugar Mill, with early Barbadian design; the 48-room Captain's Quarters, with its Captain's Table restaurant and Broadside Bar; 32-room L'Estancia's Spanish-adobe theme, including El Comedor restaurant and La Cantina bar; another Barbadian motif is the 48-room Pringle's, named after Rachel Pringle, Barbados's legendary madam; Little Bristol House, with 56 rooms of nautical and British navy decor; or, finally, South American Indian decor in the 32-room Calabali, with its Trawlers seafood restaurant open in winter season.

Willie Watersports on the beach offers everything from glass-bottom boat rides to scuba-diving instruction. This is one of the best operations on Barbados for things aquatic, with special picnic cruises along the coast. Heywoods Par 3 Executive 9 course keeps golfers in the swing on vacation, while five floodlit tennis courts and two glass-backed, air-conditioned squash courts rank among the best on Barbados.

All guests enjoy free daytime tennis and water sports (except scuba and special events). Golf-greens fees are $8.

Squash-court use is $8 per hour. All guests have free admission throughout their stay at the Club Miliki disco.

Suites $380 (for two), studios with kitchenette $225, doubles with ocean view $225, MAP $45 additional per day. For information, contact International Travel and Resorts (800–223–9815).

Restaurants

The ambience of Barbados restaurants can be as romantic and intimate as a candlelight dinner by the sea with a piano player providing soft melodies in the background—or as raucous as a wild, rum-soaked night, dancing between drinks and steak barbecue on the *Jolly Roger* or the *Bajan Queen*. Counting small, informal seaside perches, jacket-and-tie dining rooms, and everything in between, Barbados has about 100 places to eat, and deciding which to try is going to be a matter of individual cravings.

From December until May, every worthwhile restaurant is open and at its best, hoping to please the peak-season traveler and win him as a repeat customer. This is also the busiest and most formal time of year, and visitors should call ahead to make reservations, especially in Bridgetown and St. James. Many restaurants have dress codes: although most do not require jacket and tie, they will expect very smart casual dress for dinner, and very few—

aside from beachfront eateries—will allow anyone inside in shorts or jeans and T-shirts. Furthermore, there are still restaurants, particularly smaller local establishments, which do not accept credit cards.

BARBADIAN CUISINE

Barbados has excellent Continental, French, nouvelle, Chinese, and Creole cuisine for you to choose from, as well as some chummy places where you can enjoy English pub-style fare and camaraderie. But don't leave the island without sampling traditional Bajan dishes at least once. Many hotels have special "Bajan Night" buffets, usually with some kind of entertainment, live band, or floor show with local performers. If that's not your kind of dining, Barbados has many moderately priced restaurants which offer superior local fare—**Brown Sugar** (lunch only) in Aquatic Gap, the **Ocean View Hotel** in Hastings for Sunday buffet by the sea, the **Barracks** at the Island Inn in Aquatic Gap, the **Waterfront Cafe** and the **Recess** in Bridgetown, and **David's Place** in Christ Church are on this year's perferred list.

Today's Bajan dishes have evolved from a heritage of Indian, African, English, Dutch, and other West Indian cuisines. What results is an unusual selection of creations which you won't find on other islands unless a Barbadian is in the kitchen. The national dish is a variation on an African recipe, combining couscous (a mixture of corn meal, okra, and seasonings) and saltfish (salted dried cod, soaked before cooking). Jug-jug is a Christmas dish which combines salt beef, pigeon peas, onion and other seasonings, and corn flour; Pepperpot is either a soup or a filling stew, depending on what's in it, but the Bajan version has pork, chicken, beef, old duck, oxtail with the skin on, pigtails, and salt beef. Cassareep is a preservative made from the cassava, a root crop, and is all-important in the pepperpot, as are peppers. The stew originated with the Arawak Indians; everything their hunters returned with was added to the fire. (Some Bajans claim that their families have kept a pepperpot going for more than a hundred years!)

July and August is the season for breadfruit, which tastes like a slightly sweet potato, and can be boiled, baked, steamed, roasted, fried, or made into salad. Cho-cho (a mild green squash also called christophene), peas, yams, and pigeon peas round out the list of Barbadian vegetable staples.

Fish and seafood are local favorites. Flying fish, fried, sautéed, or steamed with local "green seasoning" (a mixture of hot pepper, scallion, marjoram, lime, garlic, parsley, thyme, and vinegar) is a delicacy with a mild flavor you won't have tried elsewhere. Except in midsummer, kingfish, dolphin (the fish, not the mammal), and tuna appear on local menus. Caribbean lobster is most common in the summer months, but available here year-round.

Bajan pepper sauce is legendary: the yellow, innocuous-looking mixture found on many tables is actually a concoction of scotch bonnets, scallions, turmeric, mustard, vinegar salt, and garlic which "cooks" for at least a few weeks before it's used. It is very tasty on everything from eggs to fish, but it's *very* hot as well, and if you overdo your dose by even a few drops, you'll need oxygen. Never get pepper sauce on any delicate membranes like the area around your eyes—it will sting violently.

One word of caution about fish. Barbadians eat barracuda as casually as Americans eat cod, and many locals swear that this species is not poisonous in local waters. But those who have traveled through the islands, particularly the Leeward Islands, the Western Caribbean, and the Bahamas, fear barracuda as a source of a terrible disease called *ciguatera* or fish poisoning. Cases in Barbados are rare—but travelers might not want to take the risk.

Most restaurants begin serving dinner between 6:30 and 7:30 P.M. and take last seatings at 9:30 P.M. A few will seat you as late as 11 P.M. Your bill will include a 5% Government tax and normally a 10% service charge—ask if you're unsure. If you feel the service and food deserve a better tip, you can consider leaving more.

What you pay will vary as dramatically as the eating establishments of the island. Barbados has some exceedingly formal dining rooms, where you'll need a graduate degree in French to read the menu, and shouldn't expect to pay less than $150 for two. On the other hand, you could pay as little as $5 for a filling meal of soup and *roti* (curried meat and vegetables rolled into a flour tortilla—a "West Indian burrito") and a few cold Banks beers at a small seaside snack shop, or about the same for a fried flying-fish sandwich with slaw and fries. Lunch is always considerably cheaper; at better restaurants, $20 is not an unusual tab for one. If you have any questions about prices, ask; most restaurants quote in BDS, some also in U.S. dollars.

Some hotels have the Modified American Plan (MAP), which offers breakfast and dinner daily for about $50 per person. Some of the better resorts include the MAP in their room rates. Other hotels offer dine-around plans, giving you one night each at cooperating restaurants; check with the front desk when you arrive.

ST. JOSEPH

Bathsheba's **Atlantis Hotel** (433–9445) has a long tradition of local Bajan food and lots of it, with fresh fish from Tent Bay and chicken the house specialties. This is a long drive from the west coast, especially at night along poorly lit minor roads. The Sunday-noon buffet is always a hit, with a huge variety of local dishes to sample; lunches are inexpensive and the breeze-cooled coast of the Atlantic provides a genuine Bajan "country" setting. Buffet lunch about $15. Call ahead for Sunday reservations.

In Cattlewash, the **Kingsley Club** (433–9422), an inn

overlooking the Atlantic, has Brazilian and Haitian art work on the walls, heavy foliage outside open windows, and blue and white wicker furnishings that create a bright, relaxed setting. Local businessmen lunch here on weekdays, and eavesdropping can be fun. The fresh fish—whether it's dolphin or flying fish—always seems perfect. The pumpkin and pepperpot soups are outstanding, as are the desserts, especially the coconut pie.

ST. PHILIP

You may want to return to Sam Lord's Castle at night just for the atmosphere. The Marriott's resort has three restaurants, but the most elegant is the **Cobblers Reef,** with continental cuisine in a lovely cliff-top setting. Entrees begin at $15. The real experience at Sam Lord's is the weekly castle banquet in the mansion, an expensive but memorable experience. Call 423–7350 well in advance for reservations.

At the **Crane Hotel** restaurant (423–6220), also in a cliff-top setting on the Atlantic coast, the dining area specializes in fresh lobster and chubb, with a good table d'hôte menu nightly for about $35. The $25 Sunday brunch is an event. Reservations are always essential here.

CHRIST CHURCH

One of the best restaurants in Barbados is in the **Windsor Hotel** in Hastings, Christ Church. Starters are smoked salmon and caviar, escargot, foie gras, a traditional onion soup. Among the chef's special dishes, which change frequently, are rack of lamb, duck à l'orange, tournedos Rossini, filet mignon with a choice of three sauces. There are French wines, champagnes, taped music, and flowers on every table. Reservations are a must: 436–2967.

The **Ocean View** restaurant in the Ocean View Hotel, Hastings Road, Christ Church (427–7821), has a clublike feeling for guests and the local movers and shakers who come to lunch and to gossip. In the main dining room you'll find masses of flowers everywhere, soft pink table coverings, and a staff that is more "family" than service people. The menu changes daily over a three-week period; the truly special "specials" are sauteed chub, snapper soufflé, chicken curry with six condiments, filet mignon, grilled lobster, and fresh Bajan fish deep fried with tart limes and secret sauce. Desserts include a guava Pavlova (merengue and ice cream around fresh guava). On Sunday the Xanadu Room, at ocean level, is a special spot to brunch and beach.

Josef's in St. Lawrence (428–3379), a traditional favorite, offers a sophisticated menu: a coquille in Mornay sauce, seafood crêpes, filet of dolphin or snapper sautéed with capers, tournedos bordelaise in a wine sauce. Josef sold the restaurant recently; there may now be a new chef. Dinner is about $20–$30. Reservations are required.

If you don't feel like getting dressed up, but still want a change of atmosphere and good food, go to **T.G.I. Boomers** (428–8439), a St. Lawrence Gap watering hole whose house specialty is a 16-ounce daiquiri. This is Barbados's only American/Bajan venture, offering a satellite TV dish for guests. It's more a place to meet and greet than a place to dine. Dinner prices run $6–$12. Open 8 A.M.–midnight.

Also in St. Lawrence Gap, **Pisces** (428–6558) has long been known for superb seafood—particularly a good garlic shrimp dish—and its romantic setting. Lobster tail is predictably good here, and entrees are $12–$20. Dinner 6:30–10 P.M. Reservations suggested. Nearby is **Witch Doctor** (428–7856), another popular haunt because of its unusual tropical decor and excellent value for steak, shrimp, fish, beef, and curries, and a large salad bar. Dinner 6:30–10:00 P.M.

Two restaurants in Christ Church can alleviate any pangs you might have for Italian food. **Luigi's** (428–9218) in St. Lawrence Gap is the oldest, a cozy little restaurant full of curios and with a congenial staff. Nightly table d'hôte runs about $20, entrees begin at $10. **Da Luciano** (427–5518) in Hastings offers à la carte dining nightly in an old Barbadian Great House, set in lovely gardens with fountain and statues. They also have filling specials a few times each week in season.

ST. MICHAEL

The buffet Bajan lunches, $16 on weekdays, are legendary at the **Brown Sugar** (426–7684) in Aquatic Gap, where a steel band plays during the Planter's Buffet. In a quaint old house shaded by towering trees, waitresses in traditional Bajan dress offer good friendly service, as well as advice to those unfamiliar with Bajan food. Seafood is always good here, as are the pumpkin soup and fish chowders. Dinner entrees are $15–$30. Lunch Monday through Friday, noon–2 P.M.; dinner Monday through Saturday, 6:30–9:30 P.M.

Down the road at the new Grand Barbados Beach Resort, two restaurants have quickly established themselves as among Barbados's best. **The Schooner,** at the end of the pier which stretches out over Carlisle Bay, offers excellent value and fine seafood for lunch or dinner, with a non-seafood special during each serving. The buffet has three entrees, and a staggering variety of other dishes such as salads and appetizers. Lunch $14; dinner $19. For elegant, romantic dining, the **Golden Shell** (426–0890) is decorated with Tiffany glass windows, plush velvet upholstery, and elegant furniture. The chef and staff turn out five-star creations, specializing in tableside flambé cookery and roasts carved at your table. Jacket and tie; reservations a must. Entrees very expensive. Dinner 6:30–9:30 P.M.

ST. JAMES

Every resort in this upscale parish has its own restaurant, from relaxed terraces near the beach to formal dining rooms with waiters in black tie. Dining at Barbados's Elegant Resorts—**Sandy Lane, Treasure Beach, Coral Reef, Glitter Bay,** the **Royal Pavilion,** and **Cobblers Cove**—is dressy and pricey. You can also find food worthy of superlatives at informal bistros overlooking the Caribbean at reasonable prices. **Koko's** (424–4557), in Prospect, is particularly attractive. Its tropical patio is romantic and relaxing, and the dinner entrees present some of the most imaginative creations on the island. These wear a label called "nu Bajan." This is one of the island's Gold Award winners in the annual culinary competition, and you'll quickly see why. Entrees $8–$15. Monday through Saturday dinner 6:30–10:00 P.M.

When **Raffles** opened its well-decorated doors in the late 1980s, it became an instant success and one of kickiest places in town. The safari decor is backdrop to an unusual menu that may include blackened fish with lemon butter, curried shrimp, and baked chicken with mango curry. The owners call their cheesecake "sunsational." Reservations required at this hideaway in Holetown, St. James (432–6557 or 432–1280).

The casual elegance of **La Cage aux Folles** (432–1203), located in Payne's Bay, is equally inviting. From December until May, their four-course gourmet dinner, with several choices in each course, is one of the best values in Barbados at $40. Entrees may include filet mignon with Bearnaise sauce or poached dolphin in champagne and herbs. Delicious soups, unusual appetizers—try smoked salmon with a shot of iced Stolichnaya—and fine pastries at the end, all with a Franco-Oriental twist, make this a memorable dining experience. Reservations and decent clothing required. Dinner 7:00–10:00 P.M.

Very casual—and very good—the nearby **Bamboo Beach Bar** (432–0910) is beloved of local expats, especially the Brits, who flock here for 5:00–7:00 P.M. Monday through Friday happy hours. Fresh seafood, from poached flying fish to dolphin, is always available here, and portions are generous, but Caribbean lobster is the favorite among regulars. Open for lunch; reservations are recommended for dinner. Dinner entrees average $9–$13. Open daily 10 A.M.–11 P.M.

Noelle's (432–6159) is a charming, intimate dinner-only spot just before the small viaduct leading to St. Peter

in Holetown. Family-owned and operated, it boasts a delightful atmosphere—fresh white decor, including linen-
covered tables perfectly set with china and formal array of
utensils, complemented by a profusion of green plants and
candlelight. Nouvelle cuisine with a West Indian flavor is
the menu here, and fresh local fish is the star. Excellent
tropical drinks and wine list. Entrees start at about $18.
Dinner 6:30–9:30 P.M., except Tuesdays.

   Chateau Creole (422–4116), in Porters near Glitter
Bay, is a long-time favorite for its romantic, century-old
ambience and excellent service. Classic Creole cuisine,
from seafood gumbo and Creole soups to a variety of
shrimp, chicken, and beef Creole dishes. Reservations a
must. Four course dinner $20–$30. **Reids** (432–7623) on
Highway 1, a longtime local favorite, has an attractive decor
and a somewhat timid Continental menu; the fresh fish,
steak, and chops may be the best selections. Prices begin at
$15. Dinner 7:00–10:00 P.M.

   The grande dame of dining in Barbados for the past 17
years has been the **Bagatelle Great House** (426–0666) in
St. Thomas. The old house, originally owned by the Earl of
Carlisle, dates from the 17th century. Today the restored
dining rooms create an atmosphere of elegance and romance. Make reservations well in advance, especially in winter. Dress is formal. The five-course dinner offers a full
choice from the à la carte menu, with specialties like crab
Amontillado, West Indian polpette, rack of lamb, tournedos, and many fresh seafood creations. Dinner about
$80, served 6:30–10:00 P.M.

Rum

According to local lore, the potion got its name in the 17th
century, as described in a letter written by an English
visitor. "The cheife fudling they make in the Island is Rumbullion, alias Kill Divill, and this is made of the sugar cones
distilled, a hot, hellish and terrible liquor." "Rumbullion",
later shortened to "rum," was actually a Devonshire term
meaning "uproar"—easily understood by those who have

consumed too much. But today, Barbadian rum is considered some of the finest in the world, and a drink of epicureans, not rapscallions. It became an important export back in the mid-1700s, when it was a valuable commodity in the slave-trading market and enormous quantities were sold to North America. The plantation owners' table of equivalents was simple and profitable: 1 acre of land = 10 tons of cane = 1 ton of sugar = 30 gallons of rum.

Rum remains an important export for Barbados. There are currently six brands distilled in Barbados, the most popular of which are Mount Gay and Cockspur.

The **Mount Gay Distillery** (435–6900) now offers tours every Wednesday lunchtime, where tourists can learn more about the rum-making industry. "Where The Rum Comes From" includes a look at the traditional craft of the "coopers", an explanation of the traditional blending process, a tour of the distillery, and free rum drinks from an open bar, including an assortment of Mount Gay concoctions, topped off with a buffet lunch.

Those with friends on the island will more than likely get an opportunity to try real Bajan rum punch. This smooth, simple, and delicious drink is made according to this recipe: one of sour (lime juice), two of sweet (sugar syrup), three of strong (dark rum), four of weak (water), and five drops of bitters. Top with freshly grated nutmeg, shake, and serve over ice.

Remember that in Barbados "rum" means dark rum. If you want the (imported) white stuff, you'll have to ask for it, and you won't endear yourself to the locals. If the very thought of rum makes your stomach turn, try an ice-cold Banks, the award-winning local beer. Yachtsmen swear by it as a breakfast treat.

Nightlife

Island nightlife can be as sophisticated as a quiet piano bar in one of the resort hotels or as raucous as a late-night jazz session in Bridgetown's legendary Waterfront Cafe at the end of the Careenage and, in the second story, the dusk-to-dawn Warehouse Disco, two of the hottest night spots on the island. For incorrigibles, there is always the never-closed Baxter's Road, a jumble of rum shops, snack shacks, and street vendors offering fresh flying fish until the wee hours. The "in" spot for political and social gossip is Enid's; the Pink Star has occasional jazz groups that jam into the morning hours.

Between Christmas and Easter most big hotels have something special scheduled every night, often specialty buffets with floor shows or live bands. Even during summer months, most have entertainment two or three nights a week. Check the knowledgeable *Ins and Outs of Barbados*, distributed free at hotels.

Talk to some Barbadians. They're not only a great source of information on "what's hap'nin' ," but also fine company if you'd like to see nighttime Barbados as the locals know it. Local dances on weekends, known as "brams," are where you'll find the people of the island cutting loose, and you may be invited to one if you make some Bajan friends, or find a taxi driver who knows where one is being held.

After-dark dress is generally casual on Barbados, but at the better hotels and discos along the St. James and St. Peter coast, "smart casual" is more appropriate. During winter season, some establishments require jackets for men and dresses or skirts and blouses for women. Shorts are unthinkable and unacceptable.

DINNER SHOWS

Cuisine is not the strong point of the dinner show presentations; those who care deeply about food may prefer to make a show reservation only and dine elsewhere.

Plantation Tropical Spectacular II, in the Plantation and Garden Theatre on St. Lawrence Road, features the folklore and music of Barbados in song and dance, with a cast of 30 in flamboyant costumes. Lots of Caribbean music is provided by the Cockspur Steel Band during the Bajan buffet dinner. Tuesdays at 6 P.M.; about $33 per person (428–5048).

1627 and All That, in the Barbados Museum's open courtyard, is a long-popular folkloric show tracing the early heritage of Barbados. Visitors can also view the museum's galleries before buffet dinner and show. Sundays and Thursdays; about $33 per person. (436–6900).

Barbados Barbados, at the Balls Plantation, is a funny musical comedy giving an irreverent look at 18th-century Barbados, based on the life of the island's first hotelier and madam, Rachel Pringle. Dinner, open bar, and show. Tuesdays; about $33 per person (435–6900).

Barbados By Night Calypso Cabaret Show, at the Plantation Restaurant, features top local bands playing calypso, reggae, soca, and jazz, along with colorfully costumed dancers performing ever-popular routines of fire-eating, limbo, and glass-dancing. Guests participate in the limbo contests for sprains and prizes. Dinner, drinks all evening, and dancing after the show. Mondays and Fridays; about $28 per person, $12.50 for drinks and dance only.

Night of the Buccaneers, at the Hilton International, is a pirates' party which begins in historic Old Fort Charles with a rum-punch social and continues with a buccaneers' barbecue featuring a great spread of traditional Caribbean dishes, lobster, and ribs. The show includes Barbadian dances by the Country Theatre Workshop, fire-eating and limbo displays, and dancing afterwards to a steel band. Thursdays at 6:30 P.M.; about $30 per person (426–0200).

Here is Barbados, also at the Hilton, features Barbados's leading folk group, Sing Out Barbados, presenting scenes from Bajan life, such as market day, and a cast of colorful historical characters in a very entertaining fashion. Includes international buffet dinner. Sundays at 7 P.M.; about $27 per person (426–0200).

CLUBS AND DISCOS

The **Xanadu Follies** in the Ocean View Hotel on Hastings Road, Christ Church, is the genuine article, a professional review with pizzaz. And the cuisine is some of the best in Barbados. Guests have the option of reserving for dinner or just the show. Dinner at about 8 P.M., showtime at about 10 P.M. (427–7821).

The **Ship Inn,** St. Lawrence, Christ Church (428–9605), is one of Barbados's great gathering spots for the jeans crowd. Local bands play Wednesday through Friday, with occasional impromptu sing-along sessions on other nights.

The Waterfront Cafe, the Careenage, Bridgetown (427–0093), is a charming wharfside watering hole for daytime and evening visits, with live jazz Monday through Saturday nights and special appearances by other bands. Just upstairs is one of the liveliest nightspots on the island.

The Warehouse (436–2897) has a lively ambience, and live entertainment Monday through Saturday, with dancing until 4 or 5 A.M., depending on the crowd. The name reflects the decor. The Storeroom Lounge next door offers a quiet retreat for a drink between dances.

Harbour Lights, Bay Street, St. Michael (427–9772), is a long-time favorite of local and visiting partygoers. "Hot" music groups perform on a changing basis, and afterward late-night snacks are sold on the beach.

The Village Disco, in the Barbados Beach Village Resort, St. James (425–1550), a west coast disco that seems to draw tourists only, is usually bustling and busy on the weekend.

Club Miliki, at Heywoods Resort, St. Peter (422–4900) is one of the west coast discos, with dancing from 9:00 P.M. nightly.

The Coach House, off Highway 1, Payne's Bay, St. James (432–1163), is Barbados's most beloved west-coast pub, drawing local crowds with its good food and chatty atmosphere, with live jazz, reggae, and steel bands. Closed Sundays in the off-season.

BARS

Bar-hopping has been a popular sport in Barbados for centuries. Within 25 years of its settlement, there were allegedly over 100 drinking houses in Bridgetown alone; today there are over 1,600 "rum shops"—down market local watering holes—in addition to the better-known pubs, bars, and restaurants. Some of the best watering holes, day or night, are found along the south coast: try **T.G.I. Boomers** in St. Lawrence Gap; the **Barbados Windsurfing Club**'s beach bar in Maxwell; **The Ship Inn** in St. Lawrence Gap; **Fisherman's Wharf** and the **Waterfront Cafe** in Bridgetown; the hot **Sandy Bank Bar and Restaurant** in Hastings; or the **Boatyard** on Carlisle Bay. On the west coast, the **Coach House, Bamboo Beach Bar,** and **Cricketers' Pub** in St. James are all popular gathering places after dark.

During winter season, look for the Merrymen, one of Barbados's most popular calypso bands, who usually play weekly at **Sunset Crest Beach** and a few other island night spots.

Year-round, **evening cruises** on the *Jolly Roger* pirate party boat are popular with visitors. The ship departs at 5 P.M., in time for rum punches at sunset. The cruise includes open bar, live music, and a barbecue dinner in a hard-partying, unromantic atmosphere. If this oceangoing Animal House appeals to you, book reservations through your hotel activities desk. The *Bajan Queen* (436–2159), a replica of a Mississippi steamboat, is another offshore night spot, with four-hour dinner-dance cruises along Barbados's west coast.

THEATER AND STAGE

If you want to experience some of the best musical and drama talent in the West Indies, contact the office of the **Frank Collymore Hall,** Barbados's modern theater-in-the-round in the Central Bank building in Bridgetown. Local and visiting musicians present a program ranging from classical guitar to Caribbean music and dance from January through May. The **Barbados Dance Theatre** season is in late April, a jazz festival usually takes place during the last week in May, and other events are scheduled each year. Call 436–9082 or watch the local paper for the program.

The **Green Room Players** and **Stage 1 Productions** stage plays throughout the year by West Indian and other playwrights at different theaters in Barbados. Details appear in the *Advocate* and *Nation* newspapers.

Index

Fodor's Travel Guides

U.S. Guides

Alaska

Arizona

Atlantic City & the
  New Jersey Shore

Boston

California

Cape Cod

Carolinas & the
  Georgia Coast

The Chesapeake Region

Chicago

Colorado

Dallas & Fort
  Worth

Disney World & the
  Orlando Area

Florida

Hawaii

Houston &
  Galveston

Las Vegas

Los Angeles, Orange
  County, Palm Springs

Maui

Miami, Fort Lauderdale,
  Palm Beach

Michigan, Wisconsin,
  Minnesota

New England

New Mexico

New Orleans

New Orleans *(Pocket
  Guide)*

New York City

New York City *(Pocket
  Guide)*

New York State

Pacific North Coast

Philadelphia

The Rockies

San Diego

San Francisco

San Francisco *(Pocket
  Guide)*

The South

Texas

USA

Virgin Islands

Virginia

Waikiki

Washington, DC

Williamsburg

Foreign Guides

Acapulco

Amsterdam

Australia, New Zealand,
  The South Pacific

Austria

Bahamas

Bahamas *(Pocket
  Guide)*

Baja & the Pacific
  Coast Resorts

Barbados

Belgium & Luxembourg

Bermuda

Brazil

Britain *(Great Travel
  Values)*

Budget Europe

Canada

Canada *(Great Travel
  Values)*

Canada's Atlantic
  Provinces

Cancún, Cozumel,
  Mérida, the
  Yucatán

Caribbean

Caribbean *(Great
  Travel Values)*

Central America

China

China's Great Cities

Eastern Europe

Egypt

Europe

Europe's Great Cities

Florence & Venice

France

France *(Great Travel
  Values)*

Germany

Germany *(Great Travel
  Values)*

Great Britain

Greece

The Himalayan
  Countries

Holland

Hong Kong

Hungary

India, including Nepal

Ireland

Israel

Italy

Italy *(Great Travel
  Values)*

Jamaica

Japan

Japan *(Great Travel
  Values)*

Jordan & the Holy Land

Kenya, Tanzania,
  the Seychelles

Korea

Lisbon

Loire Valley

London

London *(Great Travel
  Values)*

London *(Pocket Guide)*

Madrid & Barcelona

Mexico

Mexico City

Montreal &
  Quebec City

Munich

New Zealand

North Africa

Paris

Paris *(Pocket Guide)*

Portugal

Rio de Janeiro

The Riviera *(Fun on)*

Rome

Saint Martin &
  Sint Maarten

Scandinavia

Scandinavian Cities

Scotland

Singapore

South America

South Pacific

Southeast Asia

Soviet Union

Spain

Spain *(Great Travel
  Values)*

Sweden

Switzerland

Sydney

Tokyo

Toronto

Turkey

Vienna

Yugoslavia

Special-Interest Guides

Bed & Breakfast
  Guide: North America

Health & Fitness
  Vacations

Royalty Watching

Selected Hotels of
  Europe

Selected Resorts
  and Hotels of the U.S.

Shopping in Europe

Skiing in North
  America

Sunday in New York